**Income Flows in Urban
Poverty Areas**

Income Flows in Urban Poverty Areas

A Comparison of the Community Income Accounts of Bedford-Stuyvesant and Borough Park

Richard Lance Schaffer
Economic Consultant,
Bedford-Stuyvesant
Restoration Corporation

Lexington Books
D.C. Heath and Company
Lexington, Massachusetts
Toronto   London

Library of Congress Cataloging in Publication Data

Schaffer, Richard Lance.
  Income flows in urban poverty areas.

  Originally presented as the author's thesis, New
York University.
  Bibliography: p.
  1. Income—Brooklyn.   I. Title.
HC108.B7S3   1973   339.2'09747'23   72-12562
ISBN 0-669-85779-3

Contents

List of Figures

List of Tables

Introduction

This book is my recently completed doctoral thesis in economics on the measurement of income flows at the community level. As far as I know, it is the first published study of its kind, and like any initial exploration, it is just a beginning. Since I completed the manuscript some six months ago, I have had many new thoughts on its empirical contents as new sources of primary data have surfaced, the uses of previously discovered sources have become more evident, and alternative formulations of the community income accounts have suggested themselves. At the same time, continued readings of the thesis have revealed sections of the accounting structure that can be improved, as well as some additional problems with certain primary data sources. This is all part of the natural research process of trial and error, leading to improved research methods and increased awareness of the very complex economic and social dynamics of urban communities.

I decided to publish the thesis without any substantive changes, in the hope that it will stimulate other researchers to constructively criticize it and undertake similar studies in other cities. It is important that other researchers undertake the very laborious process of discovering new sources of primary data on urban communities if we are to attempt to answer the critical questions concerning the local areas in which we live.

It is my contention that one of the reasons we lack an understanding of urban communities is that we have been unwilling to engage in the "dirty" work involved in new data collection. As a result, the professional journals are filled with neat statistical articles using limited primary data to generate meaningless empirical results. We appear to be wallowing in a "garbage-in-garbage-out" syndrome that militates against any innovative empirical explorations. The basic fact confronting urban researchers today is that they must gather new primary data if they are to advance our understanding of the component parts of the metropolis.

At the present time I am taking a small step in this direction as an economic consultant to the Bedford-Stuyvesant Restoration Corporation. Over the next year I will be seeking to develop a comprehensive set of economic and social accounts on a time-series basis for the Bedford-Stuyvesant community of Brooklyn. This book was the feasibility study for some of the approaches that will be used in my present research efforts, although my work for the Restoration Corporation will be far more detailed than what appears in this volume.

I would be remiss if I did not mention some of the individuals who made my thesis possible. My advisor, Professor Dick Netzer was of great assistance, as were the other two members of my committee, Professors Tobier and Georgiadis. Since the thesis was completed without any formal research grants, I must thank my personal funding source, my parents, for their unfailing support. And finally, I must thank my wife, Kathy, for having the very uncommon ability to remain silent when her husband was working.

Income Flows in Urban Poverty Areas

1 Income Flows in Urban Poverty Areas

The United States has endured four major migration streams in its brief history—European, westward, rural to urban, and black.[1] Although the black migration was the smallest of these population movements, society's response to it resulted in the creation of our nation's most urgent domestic social problem, the existence of continually expanding racial ghettos.[2] This condition has prompted innumerable discussions of possible remedies from the conservative, status quo, arguments based on an acceptance of traditional capitalist principles, across the economic and political spectrum, to the more radical theories emphasizing systemic institutional change.[3] While economists have made some rather significant studies in the last few years in an effort to bring increased objectivity to the various arguments, such discussions are still characterized by gaping holes in both our theoretical and empirical understanding of the black ghetto. As a result, most of the discussions inevitably degenerate into polemical attacks and economic "knownothingness."

A topic that is habitually raised in such discussions concerns the size and direction of income flows in and out of the ghettos, and who controls and benefits from such flows. It has become increasingly popular to view the ghetto as an internal, economically backward and exploited, colony within a larger, expanding industrial economy. Such economists as Daniel Fusfeld, William Tabb, Gustav Ranis, Barry Bluestone, and Michael Zweig, along with social theorists such as Charles Hamilton, Stokely Carmichael, James Boggs, Earl Ofari, Harold Baron, Robert L. Allen, and Robert Blauner subscribe to this view.[4]

These authors view the black ghetto as an internal colony subjected to the control of the larger white society that uses it as a "residual subsystem" for its rejected and discriminated-against people, while at the same time forcing it to house black laborers existing in

> . . . their historic position somewhere between Marx's reserve army and Cairnes's non-competing group. That is, they are an available source of labor when needed by the economy and at the same time a group set apart which can be confined to certain types of work (low paying, hard, and unpleasant jobs). They have been given the worst jobs that society had to offer.[5]

And Cairnes writes:

> What we find, in effect, is not a whole population competing indiscriminately for all occupations, but a series of industrial layers, superposed on one another,

1

within each of which various candidates for employment possess a real and effective power of selection, which those occupying the several strata are, for all purposes of effective competition, practically isolated from each other.[6]

In a qualitative analysis of income flows Fusfeld goes on to observe that

... one of the most striking characteristics of the urban poverty area is the continual drain of resources out of the area and into other sectors of the economy. Although largely unmeasured, and perhaps unmeasurable, the drain includes savings, physical capital, human resources, and incomes. ... The net result of the drain of resources from the ghettoized slum is to create a backward, underdeveloped area in the midst of an otherwise progressive and expanding economy.[7]

While it is conceded by the various authors that no urban community is autarkic, they nevertheless contend that the drain is excessive compared to other communities, that a severe "connectedness" problem exists between the ghetto and the larger economic system, and that control by outside individuals and institutions functions to the detriment of the ghetto. One economist, Barry Bluestone, concludes that the real problem is "the total lack of income generating production in the ghetto, the ubiquitous hallmark of a poor community."[8]

Authors such as the foregoing place great emphasis on the total lack of ghetto self-sufficiency; its reliance on the earnings of its chief export, unskilled labor; and the outside control exercised over its people and physical plant. They stress the sieve-like nature of the indigenous ghetto economic base and the relatively insignificant multiplier effects it permits. Recent studies of the Hough ghetto in Cleveland by Oakland, Sparrow, and Stettler [150], and of the Newark ghetto by Frank Davis [51], have confirmed the existence of very minimal multiplier effects and intraghetto business linkages. These results were to be expected not only of the ghetto, but also of other communities, as virtually all communities produce very little for strictly local consumption. This was found by Friedly and Tiebout in studies of suburban communities in Illinois and California that showed very small multipliers and linkages.[9] The significance of these results was explicitly stated by Fusfeld and Bluestone, with the latter remarking that

If the multiplier of an area fails to rise much above one, but the region is productive, exporting valuable goods and services to the outside world, affluence is assured. This is the case of the white suburb.[10]

One is left with the picture of white suburbs exporting skilled labor and valuable industrial products from recent-vintage factories, while the ghetto is forced to sporadically export unskilled labor and products from aging factories. Much of the authors' discussions are directed at the severe labor market problems of the indigenous workforce, as well as the inadequacy of the ghetto's economic base. The severe labor market problems were highlighted by the November 1966, subemployment computations performed by the Department of Labor for several ghettos across the country. A "subemployment rate" was developed to more accurately portray the severe employment problems existing in the urban poverty areas by taking into account several items inadequately treated or completely omitted from the traditional unemployment rate computations. When such factors as below-poverty-level wages, "discouraged-worker effects," undercounts, and involuntary part-time employment were considered, the ten ghetto areas surveyed showed "subemployment" rates ranging from 24.2 to 47.4 percent, with a mean of 34 percent.[11]

In addition to the severe employment problems faced by ghetto residents, the economic base of their communities is very weak. Studies by Frank Davis [51]—Newark; Oakland, Sparrow, and Stettler [150] and Cox [47]—Hough in Cleveland; Vietorisz and Harrision [210], the Mayor's Task Force [132], and the Columbia University Development Workshop [44]—Harlem; Allvine [5]—the South Side of Chicago; the New York Planning Commission [147]—Bedford-Stuyvesant, Brownsville, and East New York; and the Rust Engineering Company [176]—the Hill District of Pittsburgh; as well as general analyses by Brimmer and Terrell [28], Cross [48], Mason [131], and Flint [66] all reach the same basic set of conclusions: The economic base of ghetto communities is extremely weak in some sectors, and virtually nonexistent in others. Without going into complete exegesis of the results, it can be said that boarded-up storefronts, incompatible land uses, outside ownership of most businesses (especially the larger ones), limited indigenous employment opportunities, limited manufacturing industries, and highly personal-service oriented and marginal retail and service establishments are the key factors in whatever economic base exists in the ghettos.

Flows of income are not only affected by severe employment problems and limited economic base, but also are greatly hampered by the institutionalized racism in American society. Baron writes of a "web of urban racism" possessing two components with respect to institutional structures: (1) the city's major institutional networks develop separate, subordinated black subsectors, and (2) "cumulative patterns of reinforcement" interact between the barriers defining the various black subsectors.[12] Downs further elaborated on the nature of such racism stating that

Racism can be a matter of *result* rather than *intention* because many institutional structures in America that most whites do not recognize as subordinating others because of color actually injure minority group members far more than deliberate racism.[13]

Such institutional racism as practiced by insurance, credit, and financial institutions, real estate brokers and dealers, the Federal Housing Administration, the Veterans Administration, the labor unions, corporations, and so on, has had significant negative impacts on the income flows and economic vitality of the urban ghettos.[14]

Another area in which it is alleged that income is generated and later drained from the ghetto is through illegal activities such as policy operations and narcotics. Several commentators have mentioned the significant impact of the policy operations on the ghetto economy, with some saying it is the largest single employer in such communities. Drake and Cayton state that over 500 policy stations employing over 5000 people operated in Chicago in the 1930s,[15] and a recent study of organized crime in New York City by Lasswell, McKenna, and Manoni [115] indicates that the popularity of the numbers has not declined over time. While reliable empirical studies in this field are largely absent, the evidence from those who live in and study the ghetto is that such activities are highly significant.[16] Malcolm X concluded that "the only Negroes who really had any money were the ones in the numbers racket, or who ran the gambling houses, or who in some other way lived parasitically off the poorest ones, who were the masses."[17]

Probably the only inflow of income into the ghetto that has increased significantly in the past few years is public assistance. For example, the caseloads have increased dramatically in New York City since 1966, with the number of recipients more than doubling; even after such an increase there are large numbers of people eligible for public assistance who are not on the rolls.[18] Public assistance payments have become an increasingly important portion of the total purchasing power of ghetto residents.

Various authors have hypothesized that one of the largest, if not the largest, capital outflows from the ghetto is in the form of disinvestment in the aging housing stock. This disinvestment process is due to a number of interrelated factors including: rising operating costs in relation to rent receipts, difficulties in obtaining insurance coverage and mortgage financing, the age of the housing stock, deteriorating landlord-tenant relationships, the welfare system, and poor landlord expectations. Ghetto landlords are often faced with a classic case of the Prisoner's Dilemma game in which there is no incentive for a landlord to maintain his property if no other landlords on his block do the same. The existence of the Prisoner's Dilemma, coupled with a vicious cycle of "self-fulfilling propheses," poor expectations, and uncertainty, results in disinvestment in the housing stock through undermaintenance. Landlords may well be playing an "end-game" by "milking" their properties, as they have virtually completely discounted away future returns in favor of immediate profits. As Lowry and the game theorists have shown, under such perceived circumstances disinvestment is an entirely rational strategy for the individual landlord. While the relative importance of the various factors entering into the disinvestment decision is still a moot question, it is clear from surveys of such areas that significant disinvestment is occurring.[19]

In summary, the limited amount of theorizing on income flows in the urban ghetto has hypothesized the relative importance and direction of several flow magnitudes. The largest inflow is expected to be the earnings of ghetto residents from their labor force activity, although such earnings will be much less than the amount earned in the labor market by nonghetto residents. The economic base of the ghetto is expected to be weak, with few internal linkages, and extensive outside control; the middle-income area is also expected to have a somewhat limited economic base, although more of it will be controlled locally. Illegal activities in policy and narcotics are expected to drain income from the ghetto community, and public assistance payments are expected to constitute a significant portion of ghetto purchasing power. And finally, housing disinvestment should be much greater in the ghetto than in the middle-income community.

The income flows through the ghetto are deemed to be greatly influenced by the spatial immobilities placed upon ghetto residents by such factors as discrimination, segregation, and institutionalized racism. These factors serve to delineate the ghetto as a geographical unit for income flow analysis. Income flows are analyzed by creating community income accounts, analogous to the national and regional income accounts that have been developed in the last few decades.[20]

Ever since the early political economists in the time of Adam Smith and Quesnay studied national income schemes and balance of payments questions, there has been an interest in creating better descriptions of the aggregates contained in the national income. Efforts to create such accounts have progressed from Quesnay's *Tableau Economique* in the mid-eighteenth century, to the national income work of the National Bureau of Economic Research and the United States Department of Commerce in the 1930s, to current efforts to refine the national income accounts and develop social accounting schemes. In addition to the extensive work done on national income accounts, since the 1950s several researchers have been seeking to construct regional accounting frameworks.

The creation of regional income accounts brought into focus many problems not incurred in the creation of national income accounts, such as the definition of the income recipients, the nature of transactions, statistical and measurement difficulties, situs problems, and the type of sectoring of the aggregates that would most clearly present the income estimates.[21] Similar problems were encountered by the present author in his efforts to move down the income accounts hierarchy from the national to the community level. Income flow sectors that could be incorporated into the large aggregates at the national and regional level had to be explicitly stated at the community level. In deciding upon the sectors to be employed in the community income accounts, one had to decide upon the purpose and theory behind such accounts. The sectoring of the national income accounts was greatly influenced by Keynes' *General Theory*

[110], while regional accounts were influenced by the efforts of regional economists to provide a 'better understanding of spatial barriers to perfect economic mobility."[22]

Thus, the structure of all income accounts is greatly influenced by the purpose and theory behind such accounts in the mind of the researcher. The accounts are descriptive tools based on hypotheses of the movements of magnitudes within the economic system they seek to portray. Walter Isard has stated that "national income is a set of theories, as well as magnitudes, and there are thus as many definitions of income as there are conceptual schemes."[23] Just as the income accounts constructed for larger areas than the urban community are based on theoretical analyses of the economic system, so too are the community income accounts created in this study. The sectoring of the community income accounts is based on the previously mentioned hypotheses relating to the ghetto, and the accounts seek to present evidence as to the validity of such theories. As a result, the community income accounts do not look anything like the national income accounts that are so familiar to economists, as the nature of the critical economic sectors within the urban ghetto dictate a different form of income accounting. In order to answer some of the questions raised in the earlier portion of this chapter, the community income accounts must describe the factors of strategic importance to the ghetto, as well as the middle-income area. For example, as both communities are primarily residential, the housing sector must be disaggregated to a far greater degree than in larger area accounts, in order to answer questions relating to the hypothesized disinvestment in such communities' basic capital stock. Another example is provided by the fact that the community income accounts must make it possible to analyze the extent of the divergence between resources located within the community and the property interests in these resources, in order to better understand who controls the economic base of the community and receives the returns from the community's property.

It is hoped that the preceding discussion has emphasized the fact that just as there are many possible specifications of national and regional income accounts, so too are there many possible specifications of community income accounts. The accounts presented in this study were specified according to the initial efforts in theorizing on the nature of the economic processes at work in the ghetto, as considered in this chapter. The author hopes that the community income accounts will have the appeal that Werner Hirsch attributed to regional accounts when he stated that, "Their great attraction is that they provide a consistent methodology for the organization of information-flow systems to facilitate private and public decision-making."[24]

Notes

1. Morrill [142], p. 341. Morrill estimates that the European migration up to 1920 involved 30 million people, the westward movement about 10 million,

the post-1900 rural-to-urban movement about 30 million, while the post-World War I black movement from the South to the North and West involved 5 million.

2. For further analyses of the scope and timing of the patterns of black population movements and white responses see Morrill and Donaldson [143], Osofsky [162], Rose [173], Scheiner [179], and Spear [187]. For an analysis of the degree of black residential segregation see Taeuber and Taeuber [197]. For a comparison of black residential segregation with that faced by immigrant groups see Lieberson [119].

3. The following list of works gives a sampling of some of the proposals for dealing with the existence of black ghettos: Allen [3]; America [6]; Bateman and Hochman [14]; Ackerman [2]; Davis [51]; Doctors and Lockwood [55]; Bergsman [23]; Cross [48]; Daniels [49]; Edel [60]; Faux [63]; Gordon [78], see editor's introduction; Harrison [86, 88]; Hughes [100]; Kain and Persky [107], Kotler [111]; McLaurin [126]; Sturdivant [193]; Victorisz and Harrison [209].

4. See the following works for discussions of the ghetto as an internal colony. Tabb [196], Fusfeld [70, 71], Ranis [167], Zweig [220], Bluestone [26], Blauner [25], Carmichael and Hamilton [37], Allen [4], Boggs [27], Ofari [153]. For a general discussion of the colonial economic relationship see Balogh [10], O'Conner [152], Dos Santos [560].

5. Tabb [196], pp. 26-27. For an analysis of the reserve army see Karl Marx, CAPITAL (New York: International Publishers, 1967), pp. 628-640.

6. Cairnes [35], p. 66.

7. Fusfeld [71], pp. 382, 384.

8. Bluestone [26], p. 139.

9. See Friedly [69] and Tiebout [202]. Also see Tiebout [201] and Archibald [7].

10. Bluestone [26], p. 140.

11. United States Department of Labor [207].

12. Baron [13], p. 143.

13. Downs [57], p. 78.

14. For a small sample of the impact of institutional barriers on the economy of the ghetto see: McEntire [125]; Case et al. [39]; President's National Advisory Panel [166]; Shapiro [184]; Baron [11, 12]; National Committee Against Discrimination in Housing [145]; Weaver [213]; Abrams [1]; Helper [92]; Rapping [169].

15. Drake and Cayton [58], pp. 470-481.

16. See Cook [46], Johnson [104], and Mitchell [139].

17. Malcolm X [128], p. 5.

18. Gordon [77]. Also see Piven and Cloward [164].

19. For a conceptual analysis of the landlord disinvestment response see Lowry [123]. For another, broader, view of the process see Olsen [157]. For analyses of the Prisoner's Dilemma as applied to housing see Rothenberg [174], p. 40; and Davis and Whinston [53]. For some limited evidence of the existence

of the Prisoner's Dilemma see Smolensky, Becker, and Molotch [136]. For the experimental results of this game theoretic construct see Rapoport and Orwant [168]. For a discussion of some of the more intricate aspects of the theory see Sen [182]. A description of the "self-fulfilling prophesy" is provided in Merton [134], pp. 421-436; on page 421 it is defined in the following manner: "If men define situations as real, they are real in their consequences." And finally, for recent descriptions of the condition of New York City's housing market see Lowry [124]; and Sternlieb [192].

20. For a sampling of the efforts at creating national and regional income accounts see Kuznets [113]; Jaszi [103]; NBER [144], vol. 21: Hirsch [95, 96]; Isard [102], pp. 80-181; Hochwald [98]; Leven [117]. For a highly readable presentation of some of the limitations of national income accounting frameworks see Rubner [175].

21. See Hochwald [97] and Leven [118].

22. Werner Hochwald [97], p. 25.

23. Isard [102], p. 83.

24. Hirsch [95], p. xviii.

2

Community Income Flows

Two years ago Professor Wassily Leontief, in his presidential address to the American Economic Association, chided the members of his profession for their reluctance to develop new sources of primary data. He spoke of a "fundamental imbalance in the present state of our discipline," which resulted in "the state of splendid isolation" that economics finds itself in today.[1] He was referring to the distorted value system of economists that has led them to continually seek to develop more and more sophisticated theoretical models, while at the same time ignoring the adequacy of the primary data base needed to "test" such models. The end result of this imbalance has been that "the same well-known sets of figures are used again and again in all possible combinations to pit different theoretical models against each other in formal statistical combat."[2]

While Professor Leontief was referring to economics in general, his observations on the imbalance between sophisticated theory and primary data collection are particularly relevant for the small, but growing field of urban poverty area economics. This is not only a new field, but also one in which accurate primary data are most difficult to obtain; as a result, the researchers in the field will have to exercise continual vigilance to avoid taking the path of least resistance and becoming excessively preoccupied with theoretical constructs. This is not to say that theory is not required, for it is the basis upon which scarce resources are allocated to data collection activities. Urban poverty area analysis suffers from a lack of firm underlying theory, and thus greatly needs such contributions; however, it must seek a more balanced approach than that which currently exists in many other areas of economics.

In keeping with this more balanced approach, our first chapter sought to lay the foundations for the analysis of income flows that follows. But before entering into this analysis several points concerning small area economic data must be mentioned, with particular emphasis on urban poverty area data, even though the appendixes provide detailed summaries of the economic data used and the procedures employed in estimating the income flows.

In measuring economic magnitudes in urban poverty areas all of the inherent, and often neglected, errors in economic statistics are magnified substantially.[3] For example, the estimated undercount of the total population of the United States in the 1960 Census was 3%, while in urban poverty areas the undercount of non-white males between the ages of 20 and 44 was 20%.[4] Another example is provided by Paterson, New Jersey, which felt that it was losing millions of dollars in government grants as the result of the 1970 Census undercount of its population. It funded a household survey by a local university to "recount" its population. That survey revealed that the census enumerators missed almost 25,000 people out of a total population estimated at 170,000 people.[5] As a general rule the undercount problem is an inverse function of the socioeconomic characteristics of the population to be enumerated.

Not only are people missed, but also housing units are totally missed and those found are often misclassified as to their physical condition.[6] A recent paper on such problems reported that:

... an evaluation study of reported housing characteristics after the 1960 Census found that 57% of the occupied housing units which should have been classed as "deteriorating," had been classified as "sound" in the census, while only 34% had been correctly classified and 9% had been classified as "dilapidated." In other words there is a tendency to "upgrade" housing terms in census reports.[7]

In addition to problems of finding people and correctly classifying housing units, there are numerous other difficulties in determining magnitudes for such things as labor force participation, unemployment, and the amounts of income received by poverty area residents.[8] The efforts to estimate income are so complicated by the existence of various illegal, quasi-legal, and unreported sources of income in the ghetto that one noted economist finally conceded in testimony to the Joint Economic Committee of the Congress that "I think we should face up to the fact that we understand next to nothing about sources of income of a quasi-legal nature in the ghetto...."[9] All government estimates of poverty area income suffer from an acute inability to get accurate responses from residents as to their sources and amounts of annual income.

The income flow figures presented here are therefore estimates based on all the primary data that the author could assemble, combined with the very few studies previously done on various aspects of urban poverty area income flows and empirical work from related fields. The income flow magnitudes are considered to be the best estimates derivable from the above-named sources and must be recognized as such, as researchers have only just begun to scratch the surface of the work needed to get a more detailed and accurate picture of such flows. As the recent Nobel Prize winner, Simon Kuznets, stated in 1941 in his pioneering work, *National Income and Its Components,* "the choice is, therefore, not between present estimates and better estimates; it is largely between present estimates, inadequate as they are, worse estimates, and no estimates at all."[10]

The income flow estimates presented here will seek to shed some light for the first time on a research problem posed by Daniel Fusfeld in his article "The Economy of the Urban Ghetto" [71]. This article was one of the earliest expositions of many of the current themes in urban poverty area studies, and in it Fusfeld referred to the continual drain of resources from the ghetto as opposed to the magnitudes of such flows out of nonpoverty areas and concluded that:

Aside from general descriptive accounts, mostly of a nonscholarly nature, there are few firm data on which to estimate the income flows out of the ghettos. It is especially difficult to determine the extent to which urban poverty areas differ from other urban areas in this respect. At this stage the best we can do is sketch a noticeable, qualitative difference without being able to quantify it.[11]

The present author agrees with Professor Fusfeld that few firm data exist and the estimation effort is difficult, but he hopes that in spite of these problems his analysis takes a first step toward resolving some of the many unanswered questions about urban poverty areas and the magnitudes by which their income flows differ from those in more affluent urban communities.

Bedford-Stuyvesant and Borough Park are the two communities whose 1969 income flows were analyzed. Both are located in the borough of Brooklyn, in New York City, and are situated about forty blocks from each other.[12] The two communities are reasonably close in population and land area, as Bedford-Stuyvesant has 219,000 people living in 454 square blocks, while Borough Park has 186,000 people living in 482 square blocks; but this is where the present-day similarity ends. Both communities were prosperous middle-class areas with large Jewish populations when World War I began,[13] but after the war Bedford-Stuyvesant's population rapidly changed as blacks moved into its many tenement buildings and brownstones. Borough Park has retained its large Jewish population to this day.

During the period from 1920 to 1970, both areas had small reductions in the number of people residing within their "borders." The black population of Borough Park over the entire period has remained well below 1 percent, while it steadily increased from 4 percent in 1920 to 81 percent in 1970 in Bedford-Stuyvesant. Over the last twenty years the decennial census has shown increases in real incomes in both areas, although far greater increases have taken place in Borough Park; and after increased public assistance payments to Bedford-Stuyvesant residents are deducted from their total income, the increase in income in Borough Park compared to Bedford-Stuyvesant becomes even greater.[14]

The housing stock in Bedford-Stuyvesant is among the oldest in the entire city, built amost entirely before 1915, and consists of New and Old Law tenements and brownstones. Borough Park's housing stock was built between 1915 and 1940, and has many one- and two-family homes scattered among its multiple dwellings.[15]

The two communities were chosen because they reflect great contrasts in racial characteristics, income levels, and age of housing stock, while at the same time being of similar land area and population size. Fifty years ago they were both prosperous white middle-class communities, but today only one still is, while the other has become the heart of the largest black ghetto in the nation, an area that cuts a widening path across central Brooklyn all the way to the Queens border and has more than half a million people living within its constantly expanding borders.

While it is beyond the scope of this study to analyze how the income flows changed in these two communities over the last fifty years, it will present the income flows for the year 1969.[16]

An analysis of the complete income flow statements estimated for Bedford-Stuyvesant and Borough Park is presented on the following pages. All figures are rounded off to the nearest $100,000 to further emphasize the use of estimated magnitudes.

The critical concern of the following analysis is to depict the flows of income in and out of a given pair of communities in one calendar year. To understand these flow magnitudes it is necessary to define what is meant by income in the context of this empirical work. The concept of *community income* was developed to highlight the in and out movements of purchasing power, government services, taxes, and business activity on the community level. Inflows of community income include the various sources of purchasing power (wages and salaries, profits, consumer credit, and transfer payments), the value of government services received by the community, and the sales by local business establishments to nonresidents of the community; these inflows depict the total magnitudes of income available within the community during the year. In addition to defining inflows of community income, the outflows must be categorized. Outflows of community income include the various tax payments made by local residents and business establishments; mortgage payments and maintenance and operating expenditures incurred on the local housing stock; disinvestment in housing; business wages and other factor payments to nonresidents; savings; nonlocal consumption expenditures by residents; and "repatriated" profits from local business and real estate activities by nonresident owners. To help facilitate the reader's understanding of the community income concept, a highly simplified diagram of the major flows is presented in Figure 2-1.[17] This diagram does not show each of the flows separately, but it conveys an understanding of the general pattern.

The analysis to follow shows the community income magnitudes entering each community during the course of 1969, and the community income flow magnitudes leaving each community during the same year. By presenting the data in such a manner both the in and out movements of community income can be compared between the low-income and the middle-income urban communities, as well as the relative importance of the flow magnitudes in the various sectors within each community.

The first major sector of the inflows of community income statement is the adjusted gross income of the community's residents. For Bedford-Stuyvesant, adjusted gross income was $282.8 million in 1969. This amount was composed of the following:

Profits from local businesses received by resident owners	$ .4 million
Profits from local multiple dwellings received by resident owners	6.6

13

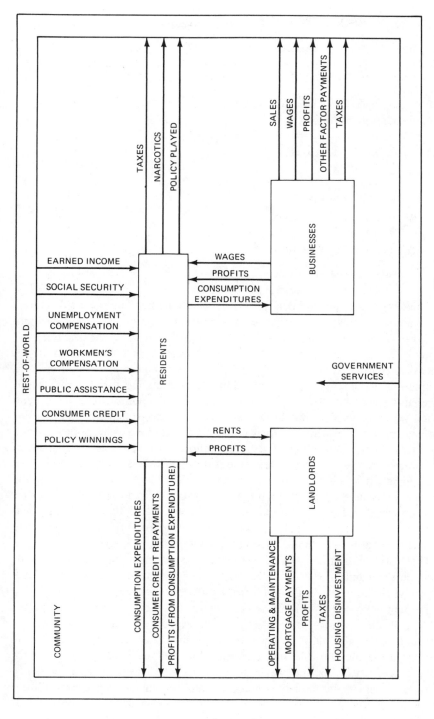

Figure 2-1. Community Income Flows

Wages paid by local firms to local residents	44.5
Other earnings of local residents	231.3
Total adjusted gross income	$282.8

For Borough Park adjusted gross income was $615.4 million, and its components were as follows:

Profits from local businesses received by resident owners	$ 4.1 million
Profits from local multiple dwellings received by resident owners	8.9
Wages paid by local firms to local residents	49.1
Other earnings of local residents	553.3
Total adjusted gross income	$615.4

The next four items on the inflows of income statement are the major sources of government transfer payments (social security, unemployment compensation, workmen's compensation, and public assistance). Following the transfer payments is an entry entitled "consumer credit extensions." While this entry is generally considered a flow of funds, it is included under the rubric of community income as it signifies additional purchasing power provided to community residents from sources outside the community. The next item, policy winnings, appears only in the Bedford-Stuyvesant statement, and refers to winnings by local residents on their policy bets during the year; policy is not a significant factor in Borough Park. The following item on the statement is government services, which shows the total input cost to New York City incurred in providing services to each community. The last three items on the inflows list are in the business sector, and refer to sales by local retail and service establishments and local corporations to nonresidents of the community and business investment. Such sales to nonresidents generate inflows of community income through the payments made to local businesses.

The total magnitudes in each of the sectors make up the inflows of community income for Bedford-Stuyvesant and Borough Park in 1969. Table 2-1 shows the complete inflows of income statements for each community.

Turning now to the outflows of community income from the two areas (see Table 2-2), the first two personal tax items that appear are individual income tax payments and individual social security tax payments by the local residents. The next outflows are those leaving the community in the housing sector. These include property taxes and water and sewer charges paid by local residents, mortgage payments by resident owners, operating and maintenance expenditures by owners, rental payments to outside landlords, and housing disinvestment. It should be noted that included in the rental payments to outside owners are $6.8

Table 2-1
Inflows of Income (Millions)

Income	Bedford-Stuyvesant	Borough Park
Adjusted gross income	$282.8	$615.4
Social Security	21.2	84.4
Unemployment compensation	8.0	4.0
Workmen's compensation	4.5	8.9
Public assistance	88.0	10.9
Consumer credit extensions	17.6	28.2
Policy winnings	11.7	–
Government services	166.5	82.7
Sales by local retail and service establishments to nonresidents	9.8	16.8
Sales by local corporations to nonresidents	237.4	237.8
Business investment	5.2	6.1
Total inflows of income	$852.7	$1095.2

million in profits from Bedford-Stuyvesant and $4.2 million in profits from Borough Park.

In the business sector of the outflows, several items appear. These are business tax payments on net income and social security; property taxes and water and sewer charges; also included are wages paid to nonresidents, other factor payments to outsiders, and profits to outside owners. The next major sector is consumption, and the first item is consumption expenditures by residents in business establishments located outside their home community. For Bedford-Stuyvesant, the $126.9 million in such expenditures includes $1.3 million in New York City sales taxes and $1.3 million in New York State sales taxes. For Borough Park, the total outside consumption expenditures of $240.3 million include $2.4 million in New York City sales taxes and a similar amount in state sales taxes. Next under consumption appear sales taxes paid by local residents on local consumption expenditures. The last item is sales taxes paid by nonresidents at local stores.

The following sector is the savings of local residents. And after this appears repayments of consumer credit, which is really a flow of funds entry in most accounting schemes, as was the case with extensions of consumer credit, but is included here because it is a deduction from the purchasing power available to the community's residents during the year. The last two items appear only in the Bedford-Stuyvesant statement and refer to the amounts of money bet on policy and spent on narcotics.[18]

In order to compare the magnitudes of specific income flows in the two communities, Tables 2-3 and 2-4 were derived showing the ratio of each flow magnitude in Bedford-Stuyvesant as a percent of the corresponding flow in Borough Park.

Table 2-2
Outflows of Income (Millions)

	Bedford-Stuyvesant	Borough Park
Personal Taxes:		
Individual income taxes	$ 37.7	$103.9
Individual Social Security taxes	13.8	29.5
Housing:		
Property taxes and water and sewer charges paid by residents	5.5	12.1
Mortgage payments by resident owners	9.7	32.4
Operating and maintenance expenditures by resident owners	7.0	24.1
Rental payments to outside owners	32.1	16.6
Housing disinvestment	25.8	5.9
Business:		
Business taxes	14.4	16.1
Business Social Security payments	4.7	4.7
Business property taxes and water and sewer charges	1.5	5.9
Wages paid to nonresidents	54.3	49.1
Other factor payments to outsiders	206.2	256.5
Profits to outside owners	14.1	13.9
Consumption:		
Consumption expenditures by residents in outside businesses	126.9	240.3
Sales taxes paid by residents on local consumption expenditures	3.0	7.2
Sales taxes paid by nonresidents at local business	.4	.8
Savings	20.2	65.1
Repayments of consumer credit	16.2	25.9
Policy played	16.7	–
Narcotics	31.0	–
Total outflows of income	$640.3	$910.1

Table 2-5 shows the flows for which the Bedford-Stuyvesant flow is greater than 100% of the Borough Park flow. The column on the extreme right gives the absolute dollar amount by which Bedford-Stuyvesant's flows are greater. (Policy and narcotics are not in the comparative tables, as comparable flow magnitudes were not estimated for Borough Park, but the flows in these two areas are surely much greater for Bedford-Stuyvesant than for Borough Park.)

Table 2-3
Ratio of Income Inflows

	Ratio of Bedford-Stuyvesant to Borough Park
Adjusted gross income	46%
Social Security	25
Unemployment compensation	200
Workmen's compensation	50
Public Assistance	807
Consumer credit extensions	62
Policy winnings	*
Government services	201
Sales by local retail and service establishments to nonresidents	58
Sales by local corporations to non-residents	100
Business investment	85
Total inflows of income	78%

*No comparable estimate for Borough Park

In relation to the middle-income community, the residents of Bedford-Stuy-vesant received over seven times the public assistance payments and had over twice as much spent on them in the provision of public services; however, in the housing sector the Bedford-Stuyvesant residents suffered their greatest propor-tional losses in comparison with Borough Park, as housing disinvestment was 440 percent greater.

The overall picture shows the middle-income community having more than $240 million more flowing through it in the year than the low-income community. It is interesting to note that both communities show "balance of payments" (inflows minus outflows) surpluses of the following amounts:

Bedford-Stuyvesant	$212.4 million
Borough Park	$185.1 million

While it is interesting that Bedford-Stuyvesant has a greater surplus than the middle-income community, it is even more instructive to see what happens to the surplus in each community when transfers and the cost of providing government services are deducted. The results are:

Bedford-Stuyvesant	−$75.8 million
Borough Park	−$ 5.8 million

Clearly, after-tax profits from businesses and housing activities flow out of the Bedford-Stuyvesant community to a much greater extent than they flow out of Borough Park. However, when the absolute dollar amounts of such profits from Bedford-Stuyvesant are compared to the absolute dollar amounts of other outflows, their dollar volume is about that of housing disinvestment, but far less than the over $200 million that flows out in local business factor payments, the over $100 million in outside consumer spending, or the over $50 million in wages paid by local firms to nonresidents. The amount of profits leaving the community is only about two-thirds of the amount of money spent on narcotics.

One should also very clearly note that the drain from the Bedford-Stuyvesant community from policy (net), narcotics, "repatriations" of profits, and housing disinvestment is over $80 million, which is almost 30 percent of the total adjusted gross income earned by the community's residents; it is also almost equal to the amount of public assistance payments received during the year. This is a far greater drain than that experienced by the residents of Borough Park.

Notes

1. Leontief [116], pp. 1, 5.
2. Ibid., p. 5.
3. Morgenstern [141]. See this book for a discussion of the often over-looked problems in economic statistics.
4. United States Department of Labor [206], pp. 15 and 2, respectively.
5. Ferretti [65], p. 29. The household survey was conducted by Fairleigh Dickenson University. The census enumerators found 144,824 people in the city, while the special survey located 170,795.
6. Taylor and Wolfe [198].
7. Ibid., p. 2.
8. See United States Department of Labor [206] for a brief analysis of some of the inherent difficulties in acquiring statistical information on urban poverty areas. Also see Gerson [74].
9. Ginzberg [75], p. 122. In a study done under Professor Ginzberg's Conservation of Human Resources Program at Columbia University by Stanley Firedlander, as reported in the MANPOWER REPORT OF THE PRESIDENT, it was claimed that 2 of every 5 adults in Harlem had some form of illegal income in 1968, and that 1 in 5 appeared to exist solely on it. This was a limited study, but it portrays the possible dimensions of illegal sources of income in the ghetto. See United States Department of Labor [205], p. 98.
10. Kuznets [113], p. 537.
11. Fusfeld [71], p. 386.
12. See Appendix A, Section 1, for community definitions and maps.
13. Ballon [9], pp. 18, 27.

14. See Appendix B for historical population and income estimates.

15. New York City Planning Commission [147], Vol. I, CRITICAL ISSUES, pp. 120-124. These pages provide excellent maps showing the age of the housing stock in various communities.

16. Refer to Appendix A for detailed descriptions of the procedures used to estimate the income flows presented in this chapter.

17. For a brief description of cash flows in the ghetto see Browne [30]. For a highly abstract presentation of money flows see Chipman [41].

18. As previously stated, policy is not popular in Borough Park and therefore it was not included. Narcotics was excluded because in the opinion of the author (after discussions with members of the Police Department and others) heroin purchases was not a significant factor in the economy of Borough Park.

3

Taxes, Transfers, and Government Services

The analysis of community income flows presented in Chapter 2 lends itself very well to answering a question of interest concerning urban communities, namely, that of the tax payments flowing from a community compared with the public services it receives. On the cost side of the question, various tax incidence assumptions must be made; while on the benefit side, there are really two separate questions. The first question is the relationship between the taxes paid out of a given community and the estimated costs incurred in providing the community with public services. The second question is a much tougher one to answer as it involves the relationship between the taxes paid out of a community and the value of the output of government services it receives. The present state of knowledge in economics permits a reasonable answer to the first question, but the second, and more important, question is far more difficult to assess.

The tax incidence assumptions made are fairly conventional:

1. All property taxes and water and sewer charges are borne by the members of the community.[1]
2. All personal income taxes are borne by the members of the community.
3. All social security payments on wages earned by community residents are borne by them; and in addition, these same residents bear the full cost of the portion of the social security taxes paid by their employers.[2]
4. Corporate income taxes are assumed shifted forward to the consumer, and since all corporate sales were assumed in the income flow analysis to be made to nonresidents, none of the corporate income taxes are borne by the members of the community.[3]
5. Unincorporated income taxes and the commercial rent tax are also assumed to be completely shifted forward, and since 90 percent of the sales of all businesses subject to such taxes in each community are made to community residents, 90 percent of these tax payments are considered borne by the community.
6. All automobile taxes and fees are borne by the members of the community.
7. All sales taxes are borne by members of the community on the purchases they make subject to such taxes.

With these assumptions in mind, the total estimated tax burden for each community is presented in Table 3-1.

23

Table 3-1
Estimated Tax Burden

	Bedford-Stuyvesant	Borough Park
Property taxes	$12.7	$ 18.0
Water and sewer charges	2.3	3.3
Total	15.0	21.3
less arrears	1.5	.3
Total	13.5	21.0
Personal income taxes:		
Federal	30.9	81.8
State	5.8	18.7
City	1.0	3.3
Total	37.7	103.8
Social Security payments by residents (including employer's share)	27.2	59.0
Unincorporated business taxes and the commercial rent tax	.6	.8
Automobile taxes and fees	.8	1.2
Sales taxes	5.6	12.0
Total tax burden	$85.4	$197.8

The specific components of the cost of public services for each community are shown in Table 3-2. The ratio of Bedford-Stuyvesant government service expenditures to those of Borough Park is shown in Table 3-3. It can be seen from this last table that, in general, it costs the city government about twice as much to supply the low-income community with public services as it does to supply the middle-income community. Tables 3-1, 3-2, and 3-3 show that the tax burden is much higher in the middle-income community of Borough Park, while the cost of providing it with government services is relatively low. Table 3-4 compares tax burdens with estimated costs of providing services in each community.

Thus, it appears that the poverty-area community contributes far less in tax revenues than the costs of supplying it with government services and transfer payments; for the middle-income community just the opposite is the case. This was noted back in 1938 by Mabel Walker in *Urban Blight and Slums,*[4] as well as in several slum-area studies conducted in the 1930s;[5] it still appears to be the case today in Bedford-Stuyvesant. Also, Camilo Marquez [130], in an analysis of all sixty-two community planning districts in New York City, found that the poorer communities generally cost the city more than the more affluent ones.

It would seem logical that the costs of providing such services would be

Table 3-2
Cost of Public Services (millions)

	Bedford-Stuyvesant	Borough Park
Police	$ 15.9	$ 7.3
Sanitation	5.4	3.4
Environmental protection excluding sanitation)	3.7	2.4
Fire	7.8	2.8
Education	64.5	26.7
Higher education	6.4	7.0
Human resources (excluding public assistance), social services, addiction services, and youth services	34.7	15.2
Health	8.2	2.2
Courts, probation, and corrections	4.5	.7
General services (residual)	15.4	13.1
Capital expenditures incurred	1.0	1.9
Total cost of government services	$166.5	$82.7

Table 3-3
Bedford-Stuyvesant: Borough Park Ratio of Government Services Expenditures

Service	Total	Per Capita
Police	218%	187%
Sanitation	159	139
Environmental protection (excluding sanitation)	155	132
Fire	279	237
Education	242	206
Higher education	91	77
Human resources (excluding public assistance), social services, addiction services, and youth services	228	194
Health	373	317
Courts, probation, and corrections	643	547
General services (residual	117	99
Capital expenditures incurred	53	45
Total cost of government services	201%	171%

Table 3-4
Tax Burdens vs. Estimated Costs of Public Services (millions)

	Bedford-Stuyvesant	Borough Park
Total cost of public services	$166.5	$ 82.7
Total tax burden	85.4	197.8
Net surplus/deficit	+81.1	−115.1
If transfers are included	121.7	108.2
Total net surplus/deficit	+$202.8	−$6.9

greater in urban poverty areas. For instance, in Bedford-Stuyvesant as compared to Borough Park, the number of reported crimes of robbery, criminal homicide, auto theft, and burglary were (in 1971) roughly three times greater.[6] The number of fires in the poorer community in 1969 was over five times as great, and so were the number of false alarms.[7] In these and many other city service areas, the demands Bedford-Stuyvesant places upon the public sector are much greater than those placed upon it by Borough Park.

A final piece of empirical evidence to support the position that urban poverty areas have more dollars spent on them than they contribute in tax revenues is provided in a recent article by Weicher [214] on the allocation of police protection services by income class in Chicago in 1959. In this article police protection per capita was regressed against such measures as retail sales, population, and income in various districts, with the result that

... the number of policemen in a district falls markedly as the median family income of the district rises. Richer districts get far fewer policemen than poorer ones.[8]

Weicher concluded that "expenditures are made primarily in poor districts, to serve poor families, who are subsidized by the middle class."[9]

This position as to the relative costs and contributions of urban poverty areas has been challenged recently by Earl Mellor [133], in his study of the Shaw-Cardoza low-income area in the District of Columbia. In this study Mellor estimated that roughly $40 million flowed out of the community in payments to government, while only $30 million flowed back in from government transfers and services. The present author feels that a more rigorous study using much more primary data than Mellor's might well lead to different conclusions as to the magnitude of the flows; if not, then the District of Columbia may be engaging in a rather perverse form of income redistribution.

The second, and more important, question of the relationship between tax payments and the output value of government services received is a much more difficult one to answer. The stumbling block in trying to come to grips with this question is that we do not as yet have a good measure of the output value of public services.[10] We do not as yet know how to measure the output of a fireman or a policeman, although an interesting study in the field of education has shed some light on the relationships between benefits in terms of the cost of services versus a measure of service output value. In a study of the Boston public school system, Grubb [80] used expected lifetime earnings due to education as the output benefit measure that was compared with tax payments. He found by using this measure (with all its imperfections) that

... nonwhites suffer most, since at every income level the benefits per person for nonwhites are approximately half of the benefits per person for whites. But even within a race, the children of upper-income parents are offered greater educational benefits than their poorer classmates.[11]

When he repeated the analysis using school expenditures as the benefit measure he found that the poor children benefited more than the rich, and that elementary and secondary schools redistributed income from whites to blacks.[12] While the analysis by Grubb is far from definitive, it does highlight some of the problems in using service costs as a proxy benefit measure, when what one ultimately desires to ascertain is the value of the received service output for the tax dollars spent.[13]

Highly complex issues of joint consumption, externalities, and exclusion costs arise in any effort to determine the output value of government produced collective goods to individuals. These issues remain, at the present time, largely unsettled.[14] However, while the effort to move from an input cost proxy measure of the value of government services, to an output value measure is hazardous, it appears logical that, *ceteris paribus*, within a given geographic community higher input costs incurred will yield greater outputs. Thus, it would appear that the much greater amount of city budget expenditures devoted to providing services to the Bedford-Stuyvesant community resulted in the community receiving a significantly higher output of such services than Borough Park.

Notes

1. Netzer [146], p. 33. Netzer's position on property tax incidence is the widely accepted one in the field, although there have been some challenges to it lately. See Mieszkowski [136] for an excellent discussion of tax incidence theory. See Oates [151] and Orr [159]. For a discussion of the Orr analysis of property tax incidence and an empirical test see Heinberg and Oates [91] and Orr [161]. An earlier article by Richman [171] presented some of the ideas employed by Orr.

2. See Pechman, Aaron, and Taussig [163]. While assumptions on the incidence of the tax depend upon one's conception of labor and product markets, the general feeling among economists is that most, if not all, of the employer's share is shifted onto the employee.

3. See Ratchford and Han [170]. The authors review the evidence on the corporate income tax and conclude that although no fixed rule can be adopted, the evidence indicates that a great deal of the tax is shifted forward.

4. Walker [211], p. 69.

5. See Hunter [101], pp. 84-85. Hunter reviews results from several studies, done in the 1930s, of slum areas in Cleveland, Boston, St. Louis, and Newark that show city service costs incurred greater than tax revenues received.

6. Burnham [33], p. 16.

7. Planning Division of the New York City Fire Department.

8. Weicher [214], p. 211.

9. Ibid., p. 218.

10. Rivlin [172] provides an analysis of the problems inherent in seeking to evaluate the outputs of government programs. Also see Olson [158], who points out the difficulties involved in seeking to count units of output and determine service provision efficiency.

11. Grubb [80], p. 10.

12. Ibid., p. 11.

13. Grubb's findings based on expected lifetime earnings as opposed to the cost of services provided leave another question unanswered: Namely, do increased school expenditures have a significant impact on public school pupil achievement scores? This is a part of the debate centering around the Coleman study showing that the quality and quantity of school inputs has little effect on achievement scores. See Samuel Bowles and Henry Levin, "On Determinants of Scholastic Achievement—An Appraisal of Some Recent Evidence," JOURNAL OF HUMAN RESOURCES 3 (1968): 3-24; also Cain and Watts [34]; and Hanushek and Kain [84].

14. For discussions of the theoretical and practical problems involved in valuing the output of government services see: Margolis [129]; Samuelson [177]; Hirsch [94]; and Tiebout [203].

4

Summary and Conclusions

A sectoral community income flow analysis for 1969 comparing Bedford-Stuyvesant and Borough Park showed significant differences in flow magnitudes and their relative importance, both within and between the two communities. The results of this analysis can be applied to the various hypothesized relationships discussed in the initial chapter of this study, to determine if there is any objective evidence to substantiate their contentions. While the evidence provided by this initial study of income flows in poverty areas and nonpoverty areas can not be definitive, as it applies to only two communities in a given year, it is still the author's contention that (as both communities are representative of their respective types of urban areas) the results have broad applicability for communities in large metropolitan areas across the nation.

But what exactly do the community income flows show? Bedford-Stuyvesant appears as a predominately black community containing some of the oldest housing stock in the entire city of New York. Disinvestment is occurring in its housing stock at a rate of over $25 million a year (in 1969), and this trend is probably accelerating at the present time. A field survey (see Appendix D) conducted in March 1972, showed over 560 vacant buildings and almost 800 vacant lots in the community. When the results of this survey are compared to results of a similar survey conducted in November 1969, it is observed that during the 28-month interval, over 150 buildings became vacant. Therefore, Bedford-Stuyvesant's 450 square blocks are dotted with almost 1400 vacant buildings and lots at the present time (excluding public housing excavations and construction); and approximately 90 percent of the current vacant lots had buildings standing on them ten years ago. Over the last ten years this low-income community has lost approximately (conservative estimate) 10 percent of its private housing units, while thousands of other units have continued to deteriorate. Various other studies show that Bedford-Stuyvesant is far from unique among poverty areas with respect to its housing deterioration.[1]

In addition to housing disinvestment outflows of some $25 million, profits leaving the community from business activity and housing rentals amounted to over $20 million in 1969. When the narcotics outflow of over $30 million is added to the housing disinvestment and profits outflows, the total of all three is approximately $75 million, or 25 percent of the adjusted gross income of the community. While these outflows assume a critical importance that is probably far greater than their dollar magnitudes indicate, due to the pervasive negative externalities they tend to generate upon community life, the two largest

29

outflows from Bedford-Stuyvesant were wages paid by local firms to nonresidents and consumer spending by local residents at stores outside the community.

On the inflow side the anticipated high dollar value of public assistance payments was found, as such payments were more than the combined total outflow of profits, narcotics, and housing disinvestment. In fact, public assistance payments were almost one-third of adjusted gross income. As expected, the largest inflow was the earnings of residents, closely followed by the sales of local businesses to outsiders. The inflow of government services valued at input cost was also very substantial, amounting to almost twice the value of public assistance payments.

The flows of income through the Bedford-Stuyvesant community were certainly not great in any absolute sense (even though the estimates tend to be conservative); and, indeed, the community appears to be rather like a sieve with a relatively small stream of income flowing through it with little remaining. While the rate of multiple-dwelling ownership was substantial, the ownership of local businesses was almost completely in the hands of nonresidents.

Borough Park's income flows have many similarities to those in Bedford-Stuyvesant; but also some very critical differences from the standpoint of community viability. Both communities have most of their labor force employed outside their borders and spend large amounts of their purchasing power at outside shopping locations. However, the residents of Bedford-Stuyvesant earn far less from their "exported" labor efforts than do the residents of Borough Park; over $300 million less in 1969.

Internal control of the economic base and housing stock is much greater in the middle-income community than in the low-income one. While three-quarters of the business profits go to outsiders, almost one-fourth accrue to Borough Park residents; this is ten times the rate in Bedford-Stuyvesant. A similar discontinuity appears in the housing sector between the two communities, and the housing disinvestment is far smaller in Borough Park than in Bedford-Stuyvesant.

The results of the income flow analysis basically confirm the often vaguely hypothesized relationships presented in the literature, and further clarify the relative importance of the various flows to each community in dollar terms. But, aside from the various estimation procedures employed, there are several reasons that the results of this study should be used with great care in seeking to answer some of the critical questions concerning the dynamics of the urban ghetto. First, the community may not value the outputs of government services it receives in an amount comparable to the input cost of such services. (This question was analyzed in Chapter 3 and need not be elaborated upon here.) Second, the question of the exploitation of the ghetto community cannot be answered from the income flow analysis. Exploitation involves notions of being unfairly treated, discriminated against, and/or not getting one's money worth in the market-place. The income flows do not show the quality of the goods and services received by ghetto residents, although various studies have presented evidence suggesting that exploitation does take place.[2] Third, the question of externalities is raised in seeking to estimate the impact of the various income flows.[3] Such critical outflows as housing disinvestment and narcotics spending (that amounted to $55 million in 1969) probably have a much greater impact on the community as a whole than indicated by their flow magnitudes. Narcotics drains human capital, while housing disinvestment drains the key physical capital of any residential community. The negative externalities generated by these two outflows involve criminal activity, fear, and overall neighborhood deterioration.[4] The total effect produced by the interaction of such externalities tends to create a vicious form of negative synergism in which the whole is much greater than the sum of the individual parts.

The income flow estimates for Bedford-Stuyvesant and Borough Park provide information for just one year, 1969, while questions pertaining to the development of such communities can be answered only on the basis of the pattern of income flow changes over a substantial period of time. But to the best of the author's knowledge, no time-series analyses of this type have been completed.

The author made some estimates of personal income for 1949, 1959, and 1969 (Appendix B), and found that real personal income rose substantially more in Borough Park than in Bedford-Stuyvesant over the last twenty years, especially when the increased public assistance payments of the late 1960s are excluded.

When the entire Central Brooklyn poverty area that includes Bedford-Stuyvesant, Brownsville, and East New York is considered, real personal income increased only 3.4 percent from 1959 to 1969, and actually declined when public assistance payments were deducted from both year's income totals.[5] It appears that not only is the relative real personal income of our nation's largest ghetto declining, but also the absolute real income as well. While there are many problems with estimating personal income in ghetto areas, certainly the presumption is in favor of a position advocating a stagnating income position in our nation's largest ghetto; and, indeed, in most of our ghetto areas across the country.

In order to better comprehend the processes at work in the black ghetto, both in the past and at the present time, researchers must begin to collect new microlevel primary data on our nation's urban areas. Parading out the same hackneyed aggregate data and subjecting it to ever more refined statistical manipulations may be the way to achieve professional rewards, but it will not begin to answer the critical questions of ghetto development.[6] All too often substantive insight loses the battle to technical expertise in the field of economics. Studies like those done by Terrell [199] and Weicher [216] exhibit the authors' obvious technical ability to deal with the intricacies of multiple regression analysis, but are severely hampered by employing the same ten-year old aggregate census data that permits urban problems to be analyzed in a very limited fashion.[7] This is not to say that such an effort to generate new primary data sources will be easy; it will not be. But such efforts will be necessary if economic studies of the urban community are to yield any truly significant results.

Regardless of the new sources of primary data that hopefully will be uncovered in the future, or the studies utilizing such data to look at income flows over time, the urban poverty areas will continue to exist for some time to come. The prospects for the immediate revitalization of such areas are very dim, and the trends toward the ghettos' declining relative (and quite probably absolute) position with regard to the rest of society appear to be accelerating. It is entirely reasonable to conclude, as Spratlen [189] did, that "underdevelopment, at least throughout the 1970s and 1980s seems destined to be the common status of the masses of nonwhites in America's ghettos."

While the trends in ghetto development do not provide the basis for much optimism at the present time, the development efforts that are now being undertaken can be analyzed within the framework of the community income accounts created in this study. The descriptive and information-ordering power of the community income accounts cannot only be used to test theories advanced by academicians, but also have a wide range of policy applications. Community planning and development efforts can be greatly facilitated by the body of information presented in the accounts; information that up to this time has not been available to urban policy makers in a consistent and usable form. The use of such accounts on a time-series basis can show the impact of various development programs, such as those undertaken by community development corporations and Model Cities agencies. The accounts can also be employed in analyzing the viability of the various decentralization schemes currently being proposed for some of our metropolitan areas. In these, and in several other areas, the community income accounts can for the first time provide urban policy makers with an objective and consistent body of small-area information upon which to base their policy decisions.

Notes

1. See Williams [218], and Stegman [190], p. 57, for reviews of the findings of special 1965 studies by the Bureau of the census in the ghettos of Cleveland and Los Angeles. For evidence on New York City see Kristof [112]. For a nationwide review of abandonment see the Center for Community Change and National Urban League [40]. A series of articles by John Herbers [93] shows nationwide trends. Also see Lilley and Clark [121]; and see the following recent government hearings on abandonment: DEFAULTS ON FHA-INSURED MORTGAGES (DETROIT), hearings before a Subcommittee of the Committee on Government Operations, December 2-4, 1971. COMPETITION IN REAL ESTATE MORTGAGE LENDING AS IT AFFECTS THE HOUSING CRISIS,

hearings held before Subcommittee on Antitrust and Monopoly, Boston, September 13-15, 1971, 3 vols. of transcript.

2. A survey of some studies of exploitation can be found in Ashenfelter [8], Becker [19]; Bergmann [22], Caplovitz [36], Case [38], Gans [73], Gwartney [81], Kain and Quigley [108, 109], Schiller [180], Thurow [200], Laphem [114], Sturdivant and Hauselman [194], McPherson [127], and Sexton [183].

3. The economic literature on externalities is extensive and only a few contributions are presented here: Bator [15], Mishan [137, 138], Baumol [16, 18], Harsanyi [89], and Sen [182].

4. For analyses of some of the effects of externalities on the urban economy see Baumol [17], Darwent [50], Davis and Whinston [53], Long [122], and Rothenberg [174].

5. The results for the Central Brooklyn poverty area are supported by data from Los Angeles and Cleveland presented by Williams [218]. For an analysis of the growth of public assistance in New York City see Burks [31].

6. Olson and Clague [159].

7. Weicher's earlier study [214] on police protection services was more in keeping with the present author's views, while showing the usefulness of regression analysis on a small area basis.

Appendixes

Appendix A
Methodology Used to Estimate Income Flows in 1969

1. Community Definitions

In the late 1960s, the City of New York was divided into sixty-two community planning districts by the City Planning Commission to facilitate its planning efforts. The community planning districts were constructed so as to best reflect the numerous historic neighborhoods that existed in each borough. While it is extremely difficult, if not impossible, to always determine exactly where one community ends and another begins, the partitioning by the City Planning Commission appears to make a good approximation of historic community borders. These community planning district boundaries are used in this study of Bedford-Stuyvesant and Borough Park.[1]

Bedford-Stuyvesant is Community Planning District #3, and has the following street boundaries:[2] West—Classon Avenue; North—Flushing Avenue; East—Broadway and Stone Avenue; South—Atlantic Avenue.

Borough Park is Community Planning District #12, and has the following street boundaries:[3] West—8th Avenue; North—37th Street, Fort Hamilton Parkway, and Caton Avenue; East—Coney Island Avenue; South—Avenue P, 65th Street, Bay Parkway, 63rd Street, 14th Avenue, and 61st Street.

As can be seen from the map of the community planning districts in Figure A-1, Bedford-Stuyvesant is in the northern section of Brooklyn and Borough Park is in the southern section; however, the two areas are only a relatively short distance from each other. At their closest points, the two areas are only about forty city blocks apart.

2. Census Tracts

The 1970 census tracts contained in Bedford-Stuyvesant are the following:

229	247	261	275	289	373
233	249	263	277	291	375
235	251	265	279	293	377
237	253	267	281	295	379
239	255	269	283	297	381
241	257	271.01	285.01	299	383
243	259.01	271.02	285.02	301	385
245	259.02	273	287	371	387

In addition, the following census tracts have specific blocks in Bedford-Stuyvesant:

Tract	Blocks
191	101 and 102
193	101 and 102
227	101, 102, 103, 104, 201, 202, 301, 401, 402, 403
369	301, 302, 303, 401, 402, 403, 404

The 1970 census tracts contained in Borough Park are the following:

110	224	242	448	464	484
112	226	244	450	468	486
114	228	246	452	470	488
116	230	436	454	472	490
214	232	438	456	474	492
216	234	440	458	476	494
218	236	442	460.01	496	
220	238	444	462.01	480	498
222	240	446	462.02	482	

In addition, the following census tracts have specific blocks in Borough Park:

Tract	Blocks
90	101, 102, 103
92	101, 202, 301
94	101, 102, 103, 201
104	101, 102, 103, 201
106	101, 102, 103, 201
108	101, 201, 202, 301
192	101, 102, 103, 104, 201, 202, 203, 204, 205
248	101, 102, 201, 202, 203, 204
250	101, 102, 103, 104
420	101, 102
434	101
500	201, 202, 301
504	301, 303, 304, 305, 306

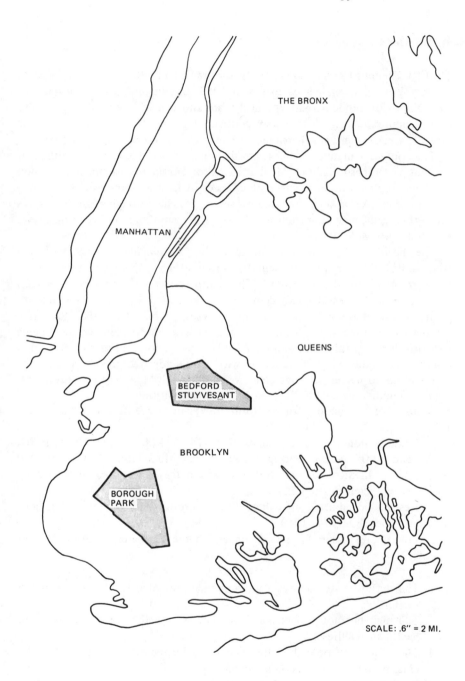

Figure A-1. Community Planning Districts

3. Adjusted Gross Income

The City Planning Commission recently acquired a computer tape from the State of New York that enabled it to match 1969 state income tax return data for New York City residents with the health areas in which they lived. Each health area is approximately three to six contiguous census tracts in size, and thus provides a manageable small-area unit for analyzing incomes.

The computer match of names with their addresses in the various health areas was not perfect, especially for Manhattan, as some residents used post office box numbers (probably referring to the addresses of their accountants) when filing their tax returns. However, the address match for the borough of Brooklyn was over 90 percent, and the match for the specific health areas in Bedford-Stuyvesant and Borough Park was excellent.

The health area boundaries do not always coincide exactly with the community planning district boundaries; therefore, adjustments were made based on 1970 population figures. (The health areas are shown in Figure A-2.) For each health area that was not totally contained within the community planning district borders, its total adjusted gross income from the 1969 state income tax returns was allocated on the basis of the percent of health-area residents living within the community planning district.[4] For example, if a health area contained 1000 residents with a total adjusted gross income of $5 million, and 50 percent of the health-area residents lived in Bedford-Stuyvesant, then $2.5 million would be allocated to the community.

Adjusted gross income for Bedford-Stuyvesant residents is estimated (see Table A-1) as $282,782,000 in 1969.

It should be noted that health areas 13.07, 14.09, 17.05, 17.07, 19.05, 19.07, 30.05, and 37.05 are all housing projects, located in Bedford-Stuyvesant, that have separate listings, but are contained within the health areas indicated by their first two identification digits.[5]

The estimated adjusted gross income for Borough Park residents (see Table A-2) was $615,389,000 in 1969.

Several points should be noted concerning the estimates of adjusted gross income:

1. The definitions of adjusted gross income presented in footnote 4 of this section.
2. The high but not perfect match of addresses on the tax returns with the health area addresses.
3. The estimation procedure for allocating adjusted gross income for health areas partially contained in a community.
4. Possible under-reporting of income on tax returns.
5. Particularly for Bedford-Stuyvesant, the nonreporting of income from illegal activities and intermittent employment where payments are made in cash.

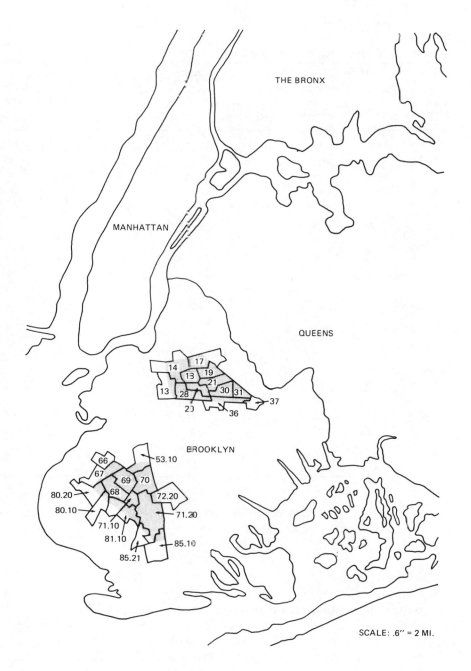

Figure A-2. Health Areas

Table A-1
Adjusted Gross Income: Bedford-Stuyvesant (1969)

Health Area	Percent of Health Area Population in Bedford-Stuyvesant	Adjusted Gross Income for Total Health Area (000)	Adjusted Gross Income Allocated to Bedford-Stuyvesant (000
13	0.50	$49,166	$ 24,583
13.07	1.00	3,007	3,007
14	0.73	18,800	13,724
14.09	1.00	8,673	8,673
17	0.65	11,017	7,161
17.05	1.00	4,538	4,538
17.07	1.00	5,588	5,588
18	1.00	15,388	15,388
19	1.00	13,716	13,716
19.05	1.00	1,119	1,119
19.07	1.00	3,699	3,699
20	1.00	24,308	24,308
21	1.00	20,608	20,608
28	1.00	41,498	41,498
30	1.00	39,338	39,338
30.05	1.00	4,696	4,696
31	1.00	32,722	32,722
36	0.62	16,524	10,245
37	0.35	20,117	7,041
37.05	1.00	1,130	1,130
			$282,782

It is highly probable that the estimates of income for the two communities are conservative, especially for Bedford-Stuyvesant.

4. Consumer Credit

An estimate of consumer credit repaid in 1969 by Bedford-Stuyvesant residents was made with the help of a special low-income area study released in January 1972, by the Bureau of the Census.[6] This study covered a low-income area of Brooklyn (Bedford-Stuyvesant, Brownsville, and East New York) with over twice as many people in it as in Bedford-Stuyvesant. (A map of the survey area appears in Figure A-3.)

This study listed the number of survey-area families having monthly install-

Table A-2
Adjusted Gross Income: Borough Park (1969)

Health Area	Percent of Health Area Population in Borough Park	Adjusted Gross Income for Total Health Area (000)	Adjusted Gross Income Allocated to Borough Park (000)
53.10	0.55	$82,175	$ 45,196
66	0.22	60,488	13,307
67	0.71	75,760	53,790
68	1.00	91,641	91,641
69	1.00	43,390	43,390
70	1.00	115,140	115,140
71.10	1.00	38,319	38,319
71.20	1.00	120,338	120,338
72.20	0.15	83,464	12,520
80.10	0.28	45,752	12,811
80.20	0.13	33,979	4,417
81.10	0.87	50,556	43,984
85.21	0.40	51,341	20,536
			$615,389

ment repayments (63.1 percent), and the number of families in each dollar class of monthly installment repayments. By multiplying the midpoint of the dollar classes of repayments by the number of families in each class, an estimate of total monthly installment repayments was obtained for the entire survey area. This monthly total was then multiplied by twelve months with the final result showing total annual repayments of $34.8 million for the area.

This total for the survey area was then multiplied by 46.5 percent (the 1970 Bedford-Stuyvesant population as a percent of the 1970 low-income survey-area population), to obtain a yearly installment repayments estimate of $16.2 million for the Bedford-Stuyvesant residents.

In addition to deriving an estimate of consumer credit (installment debt) repaid, an estimate of consumer credit extended in 1969 was required. This estimate was made with the assistance of data provided in a Conference Board publication summarizing economic data from various government agencies.[7] This consumer credit data showed an 8.8 percent increase in extensions over repayments of consumer credit for the United States in 1969. This 8.8 percent increase was applied to the consumer credit repaid estimate of $16.2 million to derive an estimae of 1969 consumer credit extended to Bedford-Stuyvesant resident residents of $17.6 million.

To obtain an estimate of consumer credit repaid by Borough Park residents the Conference Board publication was used again.[8] Installment debt (not repayments of debt) by income groups was given for the nation showing the direct relationship between increased income and installment debt for income groups earning between $5,000 and $15,000 per year. The percent of families in each installment debt class was multiplied by the midpoint of the debt class for families earning from $5,000 to $7,500 per year and those earning from $10,000 to $15,000 per year as an approximation to the median family incomes in Bedford-Stuyvesant and Borough Park respectively. It was found that the amount of installment debt for the higher family-income group was approximately 1.6 times that of the less affluent group.

The estimate of consumer credit repaid of $16.2 million for the Bedford-Stuyvesant residents was therefore multiplied by a factor of 1.6 to get an estimate of Borough Park consumer credit repaid of $25.9 million. This estimate of consumer credit repaid was then increased 8.8 percent (as was done for Bedford-Stuyvesant) to get an estimate of $28.2 million for consumer credit extended in 1969 to Borough Park residents.

The method used to estimate small-area extensions and repayments of consumer credit was extremely rough, but it was the only reasonable alternative open to the author. Of the four numbers estimated, the most confidence is placed in the estimate of consumer credit repaid in Bedford-Stuyvesant, with less confidence placed in the other figures. The accuracy of the other three estimates will obviously increase to the extent that extensions of consumer credit in both areas reflect national trends, and that national differences in consumer debt portions of families of different income levels are applicable.

5. Savings

Estimates of savings in each area were made using data from the 1960-1961 Survey of Consumer Expenditures by the Bureau of Labor Statistics that appeared in Galenson's recent article in the *American Economic Review.*[9] Savings as a percent of income for whites (9 percent) and for blacks (5 percent) were used to determine savings in Borough Park and Bedford-Stuyvesant respectively.

For Borough Park, 9 percent of adjusted gross income and transfer payments of $723,575,340 gave savings of $65,121,781. For Bedford-Stuyvesant, 5 percent of adjusted gross income and transfer payments of $404,458,996 gave savings of $20,222,950. (See section 3 for the estimate of adjusted gross income, and section 6 through section 9 for the transfer payments estimates.)

6. Public Assistance

The Management Science Unit of the Office of Administration of the City of New York used its Geographic Information System to match the addresses of

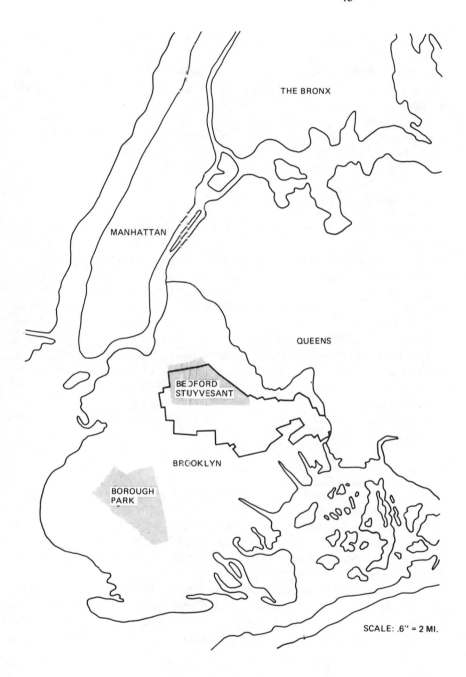

Figure A-3. Census Bureau's Central Brooklyn Survey Area

the public assistance recipients in the city with their community planning districts of residence using a tape of regular biweekly checks supplied by the Department of Social Services. As a result of this effort it was estimated that during 1969 the residents of Bedford-Stuyvesant received $87,954,050, while the Borough Park residents received $10,906,164.

Public assistance as defined in this section includes the following six categories of aid: Old Age Assistance, Assistance to the Blind, Aid to Disabled, Aid to Dependent Children, Home Relief, and Veteran Assistance.

7. Unemployment Compensation

The estimate of unemployment compensation payments to Bedford-Stuyvesant residents was derived from the previously mentioned Bureau of the Census low-income area study. In this study there is a detailed account of the number of families receiving unemployment compensation, and the amounts received by dollar classes.[10] By multiplying the number of families in each class by the midpoint of the dollar benefit classes an estimate of $17,255,500 was derived for the survey area. As in the case of installment debt, 46.5 percent of this amount was allocated to Bedford-Stuyvesant, or $8,023,808.

The estimate of unemployment compensation payments to Borough Park residents had to be derived in a different manner. As it has been a long-established "fact" that black unemployment rates are twice as high as white unemployment rates,[11] one-half of the Bedford-Stuyvesant estimate, or $4,011,904, was used as the Borough Park estimate of unemployment compensation payments received in 1969.

8. Workman's Compensation

Just as in the case of unemployment compensation, the same table in the low-income study by the Bureau of the Census was used to derive an estimate of workmen's compensation payments for Bedford-Stuyvesant.[12] For the entire survey area the payments were $11,725,750; therefore, the 46.5 percent of this allocated to Bedford-Stuyvesant was $4,452,474.

For Borough Park this figure was doubled to $8,904,948 due to the higher incomes of the area's residents and their ability to secure such payments. This was an arbitrary adjustment, but clearly some adjustment was necessary to reflect Borough Park's greater adjusted gross income.

9. Social Security

Once again the previously mentioned low-income study was used for Bedford-Stuyvesant with the result being an estimate of $21,246,664 received by the members of the community in social security payments.[13]

Borough Park's census tracts in 1970 showed almost 3.5 times as many people over the age of 65 as did the census tracts in Bedford-Stuyvesant; therefore, the social security payments received by the members of the poorer community were multiplied by 3.5 to reach the Borough Park estimate of $84,363,324.

10. Policy and Narcotics

The estimates for policy and narcotics in Bedford-Stuyvesant were derived from a recently completed study of organized crime in the community.[14] This study defined its area as the 77th and 79th police precincts in Brooklyn, an area of 281,000 people. As shown in Figure A-4, the 77th precinct is almost entirely out of the community planning district definition of Bedford-Stuyvesant; therefore, some adjustments had to be made in order to use the organized crime study findings in the present study.

The 77th precinct encompasses an area known as Crown Heights that in recent years has become increasingly identified as part of Bedford-Stuyvesant. It appears reasonable to assume that the socioeconomic characteristics of the 77th precinct are close enough to those existing in the area defined by the Planning Commission as Bedford-Stuyvesant to warrant applying the organized crime findings to the author's study. Therefore, since the present study area has 78 percent as many people as the organized-crime study area, this portion of the dollar amounts spent on policy and narcotics was used. The estimates made on this basis for the amounts spent by Bedford-Stuyvesant on policy and narcotics are shown in Table A-3.

The organized crime study is the only piece of social science research of its kind, and its estimates of criminal activity derived from police raid records, medical examiner's files, and other sources of data appear to be entirely

Table A-3

Amounts Spent on Policy and Narcotics

	Findings for the 77th and 79th Precincts[a]	Estimates for Bedford-Stuyvesant[b]
Amount bet on policy	$21,419,000	$16,706,820
Amount bet that went out of the community to organized crime	6,425,700	5,012,046
Amount spent on narcotics	39,716,520[c]	30,978,886[d]

[a]Organized crime study, 1969, Lasswell, McKenna, and Manoni [115], pp. 24, 26.
[b]Based on 78% of the precinct findings.
[c]By 6036 addicts in the 77th and 79th precincts.
[d]By 4708 addicts in Bedford-Stuyvesant.

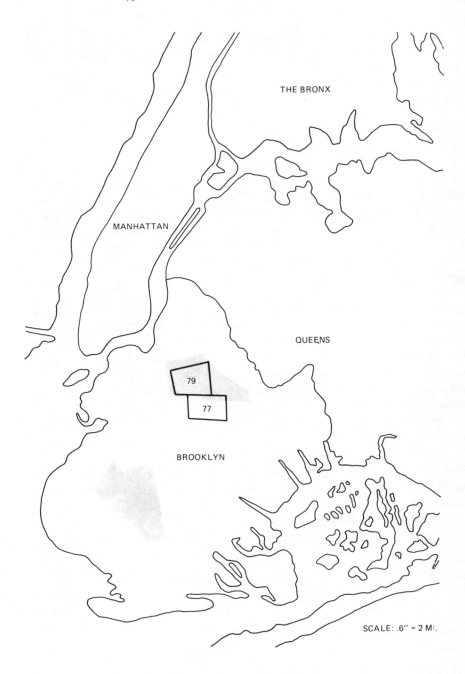

Figure A-4. The 77th and 79th Police Precincts in Brooklyn

reasonable. Much more work is needed in this research area, but the pioneering effort made by the Policy Science Center is certainly a promising start.

11. City Services

Police

The 79th and 81st police precincts "fit" the boundaries of Bedford-Stuyvesant rather well so that all expenditures for these precincts were deemed to have been incurred for the planning district (see Figure A-5).

The *Uniform Force Personnel* monthly manpower reports of the Police Department were used to determine the average number of men by rank in these two precincts in 1969. The number of policemen by rank were then multiplied by their respective total costs to the city (supplied by the Planning Division of the Police Department) to obtain a total manpower cost for Bedford-Stuyvesant of $9.1 million. This dollar amount was the cost to the city of the policemen physically on duty in this community for the entire year. In addition, there were other costs incurred in providing police services to the community.

The monthly reporting sheets, *All Personnel Assigned in Borough of Brook-lyn North*, were used to allocate a portion of the manpower costs of the Brooklyn North division to Bedford-Stuyvesant. The 79th and 81st precincts are two of the eleven precincts in this division and therefore 2/11ths of the division costs, or $2.4 million, were allocated to the community.

The police department's planners estimated that in 1969 one-half of the time spent by the Brooklyn tactical patrol force units was spent in the Bedford-Stuyvesant precincts, which added another $1.5 million.

In addition to these manpower costs, an estimate of the number of patrol cars in the community during the year, their replacement costs and life expectancies, and gasoline and repair costs added another $90,000.

The above costs came to $13.1 million.

In order to complete the estimate of the costs of providing police services to the community, it was necessary to allocate a portion of the rest of the police budget to the community. An analysis of the *Executive Budget* for fiscal years 1968-1969 and 1969-1970 showed that $73.8 million (an average of the two fiscal years was used to obtain the calendar year 1969) was left to be allocated for such items as communications, special squads, ballistics, personnel, planning, community relations, debt service, and so on.[15] This allocation was done on the basis of the number of crime prevention and control personnel at work in Bedford-Stuyvesant as a percent of the city-wide total of such personnel. On the basis of such an allocation the community received $2.9 million.

Therefore, the grand total of expenditures for police services in Bedford-Stuyvesant was $15.9 million.

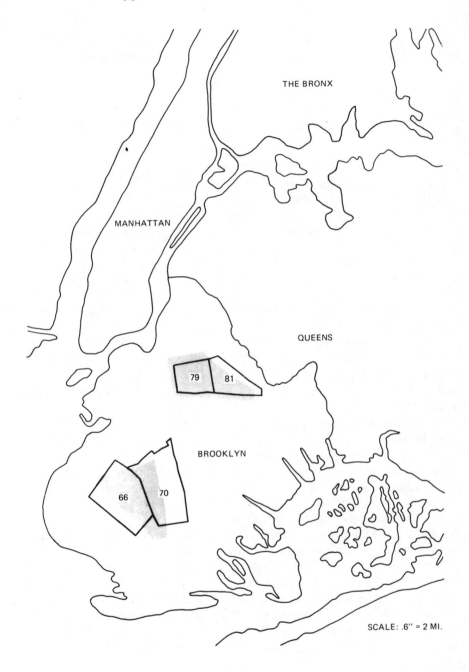

Figure A-5. The 66th, 70th, 77th, and 81st Police Precincts in Brooklyn

The procedure for determining police expenditures in Borough Park was the same as for Bedford-Stuyvesant, except for one additional complication. As can be seen from Figure A-5, the boundaries of the 66th and 70th precincts that encompass the community were not as close to matching community lines as were the precinct boundaries for Bedford-Stuyvesant; therefore, an adjustment had to be made before the previously described procedure could begin. An analysis of 1970 census-tract population data revealed that 59 percent of the total population of the 66th and 70th precincts resided in Borough Park, and this percent was used to deflate the expenditures made in the two precincts.

After this adjustment was made the allocation procedure was the same with the exception that an estimated quarter of the Brooklyn Tactical patrol force time was spent in this community. The community had $4 million as the costs of policemen physically located in it on a daily basis; $1.5 million as its share of the Brooklyn Borough South Division; $500,000 for the tactical patrol force; $68,000 for vehicles; and $1.3 million as its share of overhead costs. Total costs of providing police services to the Borough Park community were $7.3 million.

Environmental Protection

The sanitation portion of the environmental protection allocation for Bedford-Stuyvesant was calculated on the basis of data from the *Monthly Progress Report and Statistical Review* of the Department of Sanitation for 1969. The department publication gave statistics on costs per ton for refuse collection and disposal, as well as costs for street cleaning and snow removal. These costs were applied to the total number of tons of refuse collected and disposed, miles of street cleaned, and tons of snow and ice removed for the year in the community.

The same statistical source listed total manpower by sanitation district and these manpower figures were multiplied by total costs to the city per man to arrive at manpower costs per sanitation district. As can be seen from the map of sanitation districts (Figure A-6), the fit of district lines with those of the community was not perfect; therefore, as was done previously for police, the 1970 population of the community within each sanitation district was used to allocate district spending.

The total cost of sanitation services in Bedford-Stuyvesant was $5.4 million, while the cost for Borough Park was $3.4 million.

The remainder of the Environmental Protection Administration's budget amounted to $130 million, and this had to be allocated. This allocation was done on the basis of the total number of street cleaning, refuse collection, and waste disposal personnel working in each community as a percent of the city-wide total. For Bedford-Stuyvesant this meant an additional $3.7 million, while for Borough Park $2.4 million was added. Therefore, the total Environmental Protection Administration spending for Bedford-Stuyvesant was $9.1 million, while for Borough Park it was $5.8 million.

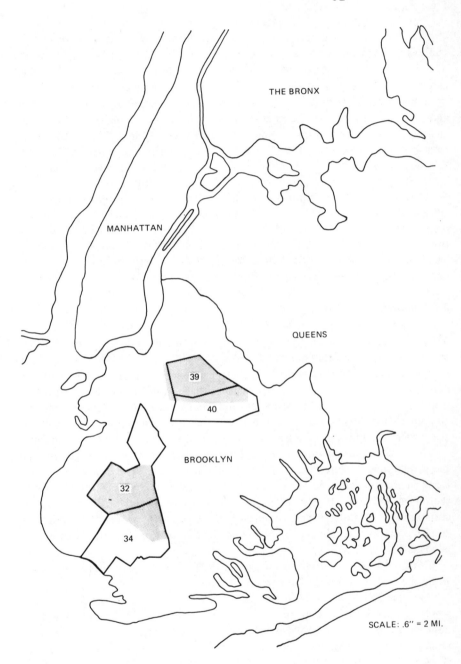

Figure A-6. Sanitation Districts

Fire

The Fire Department budget was allocated in a slightly different way than were the previously discussed budgets, since the physical location of a fire company within the community was the determining factor rather than a set of district lines. Each fire company generally services its local area, although in emergencies it may travel to other parts of the city; therefore, the number of companies in each community was used as the budget allocator. The Bedford-Stuyvesant community had nine companies located in it; Borough Park had four companies; in addition, the companies in Bedford-Stuyvesant were more heavily manned.

Allocating the Fire Department budget upon such a basis meant that $7.8 million was spent for fire protection services in Bedford-Stuyvesant, while $2.8 million was spent for such services in Borough Park.

Education

The Office of Planning, Programming, and Budgeting of the Board of Education did an analysis for its Educational Optimization System entitled the *1969-70 School Data File* that gave a school-by-school listing of numbers of registered students and mean per pupil cost of instruction. This analysis was used to calculate total instructional dollars spent in each community on the assumption that the primary and junior high schools physically located in each community serviced children from their respective communities.

The results of this analysis showed that Bedford-Stuyvesant had over 40,000 primary, middle, and junior high school students costing the city $24.4 million in instructional costs. Borough Park had just over 14,000 students costing $8.9 million.

In order to determine the per school costs of paraprofessionals and teacher's aides, a sample from the *Social Security Payroll Register* of the Board of Education of pay periods for each school was studied. The results of this analysis showed paraprofessional and teacher aide expenditures in Bedford-Stuyvesant of $1.6 million, while $170,000 was spent in Borough Park.

Cost figures supplied by the Department of School Buildings showed that in 1969 Bedford-Stuyvesant schools had $800,000 spent on their maintenance, while Borough Park schools received $300,000 in such expenditures.

High school expenditures were not as readily allocable by school location, because Bedford-Stuyvesant and Borough Park high school students often do not attend high schools within their respective community borders. The allocation of high school expenditures was made on the basis of the number of high school students in each community as a percent of the total high school population as indicated by the 1960 Census. Allocating the high school budget in this manner meant $7.9 million for Bedford-Stuyvesant and $6.8 million for Borough Park.

The rest of the education budget for the city was allocated on the basis of the 1969 kindergarten, elementary, and junior high school registered students in each community as a percent of the city-wide total. This meant that Bedford-Stuyvesant received $29.9 million, while Borough Park received $10.6 million.

Therefore, the total educational expenditure on Bedford-Stuyvesant students was $64.5 million, while $26.7 million was spent on students in Borough Park.

Higher Education

The allocation for the City University of New York was done on the basis of a survey of the freshman class done by the Office of the Mayor. The survey showed that 2.9 percent of the freshman class of the City University resided in Bedford-Stuyvesant, and 3.2 percent lived in Borough Park. The total budget for the calendar year 1969 for the City University was $219.7 million.[16] Applying the student residence percentages to the total budget gave the following results: Bedford-Stuyvesant students had $6.4 million spent on their higher education, while $7 million was spent on the students from Borough Park.

Human Resources; Social, Addiction,
and Youth Services

The total combined budgets of these areas were allocated on the basis of the percent of public assistance dollars going into the two communities as determined by the computer address match described in section 6. This match revealed that 7.613 percent of all public assistance payments went to Bedford-Stuyvesant residents, while 0.944 percent went to people living in Borough Park. The total public assistance payments for New York City were subtracted (as they were already allocated as transfer payments) from the combined budgets of these four agencies, and the remaining dollars were allocated on the basis of the above named percentages. Bedford-Stuyvesant received $34.7 million and Borough Park received $15.2 million.

Health

The basis for allocating health expenditures was a 1968 study of inpatients in municipal hospitals in Brooklyn, done by the Department of Hospitals research staff.[17] Through the use of this study it was possible to determine the percent of community residents using the Brooklyn municipal hospitals. By applying these percentages to the budgets of these hospitals it was possible to allocate $5.3 million to Bedford-Stuyvesant and $1.4 million to Borough Park. These municipal-hospital expenditures for residents of the two communities were then expressed as a percent of the total New York City hospital budget for 1969, and these percents were used to allocate the remainder of the health budget. Thus, an additional $3 million was allocated to Bedford-Stuyvesant and $800,000 to Borough Park.

The total health expenditures for Bedford-Stuyvesant were $8.2 million, while the total for Borough Park was $2.2 million.

Courts, Probation, and Corrections

The total dollar amounts spent on courts, probation, and corrections was allocated to the two communities on the basis of an analysis of precinct arrests for criminal homicide, burglary, auto theft, and robbery made by the *New York Times* for 1971.[18] This analysis showed a total of 1770 arrests in Bedford-Stuyvesant and 252 arrests in Borough Park. Of all city arrests, Bedford-Stuyvesant had 4.00 percent, while Borough Park had 0.59 percent. When these percents were multiplied by the total budgets these services are shown to have cost the city $4.5 million for Bedford-Stuyvesant and $700,000 for Borough Park.

Other Services

The remainder of the New York City budget was split into two categories: city-wide services and Brooklyn services. The first category included such areas as the City Council, Office of the Mayor, Board of Elections, Department of Consumer Affairs, City Planning Commission, Department of Investigation, Finance Administration, Economic Development Administration, etc. The second category included the Brooklyn Borough President, Public Library, Museum, District Attorney, and so on. The total dollar amounts of the services in the two categories were a relatively small amount of the total city budget, as together they were significantly below the Police Department budget.

The first category was allocated on the basis of each community's share of the city population. The second category was allocated on the basis of each community's share of Brooklyn's population. This allocation procedure resulted in a total of $15.4 million for Bedford-Stuyvesant and $13.1 million for Borough Park.

Capital Expenditures

The final item in the city services section is not really a service, but a capital expenditure. To estimate the capital expenditures actually incurred in 1969, an analysis of the *Summary Statement of Fund Balances* in the Division of Disbursement of the Bureau of Accountancy (Comptroller's Office) was undertaken. The changes from December 31, 1968 to December 31, 1969 in the net warranted expense column of the ledgers showed the amounts actually spent in 1969 on capital projects in each community.

This analysis revealed that $1 million was spent on Bedford-Stuyvesant, while $1.9 million was spent in Borough Park.

Summary

In review of the city services allocation procedures used in this study several points should be noted:

1. For police, sanitation, fire, and education an estimate was made of the actual number of full-time personnel working in each community.
2. For these same services, the number of workers in each community compared to the city-wide total was used to allocate the remaining budget dollars.
3. Surveys and computer matches were used as the basis upon which to allocate hospital care, higher education, human resources, social services, addiction services, and youth services budgets.
4. The remaining services were divided into city-wide and borough services and allocated on the basis of each community's share of city and borough population respectively.
5. The *1969-1970 Executive Budget*, showing budgeted amounts for fiscal years 1968-1969 and 1969-1970 was the source of all the budget data. In all cases the average of the two fiscal years was taken to convert the data to calendar year 1969.
6. Any allocation of the costs of government services to small areas of a political jurisdiction involves numerous assumptions; therefore, every effort was taken to make the allocation assumptions as straight forward as possible. However, the previously described procedures should not obscure the fact that all such allocations are to be certain extent arbitrary.

12. Housing

Bedford-Stuyvesant

The first step in dealing with the issue of the undermaintenance of the housing stock in Bedford-Stuyvesant was to make an estimate of the amount of rent paid in 1969 by its residents. This was estimated in the following manner. The 1970

Census found 66,323 housing units in the community, of which 1,910 were either vacant, for rent, or for sale; therefore, 64,413 housing units were occupied. The New York City Housing and Development Administration's *Multiple Dwelling Report* listed 65,864 housing units in 10,728 multiple dwellings (three or more units) in the same area in 1970. The findings of both sources are very close; therefore, the assumption was made that for estimating purposes all buildings in Bedford-Stuyvesant would be considered multiple dwellings and that 64,413 housing units were occupied.

Of the 64,413 occupied housing units, some were owner-occupied and paid no monthly contract rent. To determine the ownership of the Bedford-Stuyvesant housing stock, a match was done comparing a listing of the addresses of all multiple dwellings in the area with the *Telephone Master List* of the Housing and Development Administration. (See Appendix C for the details of this match procedure.) From this match it was estimated that 51 percent of the structures were owner-occupied. Therefore, to get an estimate of the number of rent-paying occupied housing units, 5561 owner-occupied housing units (51 percent of 10,728) had to be subtracted from the 64,413 units. The total number of rent-paying units was thus 58,852.

To determine average monthly rents the number of housing units in each census tract were multiplied by the average monthly rent per tract, using the 1970 census data from the third count. This procedure gave an estimate of $89 per housing unit per month in contract rent, and a total rent bill of $62.9 million.

The match analysis using the *Telephone Master List* also revealed that 49 percent of the housing units in the community were owned by Bedford-Stuyvesant residents; therefore, 49 percent of the total rent bill, i.e., $30.8 million, was paid to them while the remainder, $32.1 million, went to outside landlords.

The next step in deriving an estimate of housing undermaintenance was to determine what landlords should have spent to properly maintain their property and still receive an adequate rate of return. This was done using a variant of the maximum base rents (MBR) formula recently developed for the New York City rent control system.[19] The MBR system is currently in use to determine the maximum allowable rents on the rent-controlled housing stock in the city. It consists of five components: real estate taxes, water and sewer charges, operating and maintenance expenses, vacancy and collection losses, and return on capital value.[20] The real estate tax and water and sewer charge components are based on actual payments by the property owner, the operating and maintenance expense allowance is based on a formula, the vacancy and collected loss allowance is set at 1 percent of total MBR, and the return on capital value is a legislated amount including allowances for interest, amortization, and profit. For a complete understanding of the MBR system the reader is advised to consult the above cited publication.

The MBR procedure for Bedford-Stuyvesant went as follows:

1. The $208.2 million assessed value of residential property was multiplied by the calendar year 1969 Brooklyn tax rate of .054017 (average of the tax rates for fiscal years 1968-1969 and 1969-1970) to obtain total real estate taxes of $11.2 million.

2. Water and sewer charges vary greatly, depending on the size of the building, number of apartments, number of stories, etc.;[21] therefore, the 1972 MBR city-wide calculations showing $220.0 million in real estate taxes and $40.4 million in water and sewer charges[22] were used to obtain a ratio of water and sewer charges to real estate taxes of 18.4 percent. This percent was applied to the real estate taxes of the community ($11.2 million) to obtain water and sewer charges of $2.1 million.

3. The operating and maintenance expense allowances were calculated by a formula taking into consideration the number of units, number of rooms, and age of the building. The formula was derived from a regression analysis

... of data submitted by 391 applicants to the Office of Rent Control for hardship rent increases in 1966 and 1967. These buildings were free of code violations and reported to be well-managed.[23]

After correcting for inflationary cost increases between 1967 and 1969,[24] the formula for operating and maintenance expenses per unit was as follows:

A basic allowance of $214.74 per apartment

> + $0.29 per apartment
> + $59.29 per room
> + $1.74 per year of building age

In computing operating and maintenance expenses the assumptions were made, based on multiple-dwelling reports, that each unit had an average of four rooms and that building age was set at sixty-seven years (the maximum allowed under the formula). It was determined that $37.7 million was required in 1969 for operating and maintenance expenses on Bedford-Stuyvesant multiple dwellings.

4. Vacancy and collection loss allowance was 1 percent of MBR.

5. The MBR system specifies that the return on capital value should be determined by multiplying the assessed value by a special state equalization rate, and then by the legislated 8.5 percent return rate.[25] The state equalization factor developed by the New York State Board of Equalization and Assessment for 1972 is 1.754.[26] This implies an assessed value to market value ratio of around 60 percent city-wide, which may be reasonable, but for Bedford-Stuyvesant the rate is too high.[27] An analysis of this question appears in Appendix C, where a ratio of assessed value to market value of 40 percent is found for this community, implying an equalization factor of 2.5. These results were later confirmed in discussions at the New York City Tax Assessor's Office.

Therefore, the return on capital value was

$208.2 million (2.5)(0.085) = $44.2 million.

The computation of MBR for Bedford-Stuyvesant was done using the following formula.[28]

$$\text{MBR} = \frac{TX + WS + CV + OM}{0.99} = \$96.2 \text{ million}$$

where

TX	= real estate taxes
WS	= water and sewer charges
CV	= return on capital value
OM	= operating and maintenance allowance
VCL	= vacancy and collection loss

According to the MBR system's criterion for adequate maintenance and return the residential property required $96.2 million, but rents were only $62.9 million; there was a deficit of $33.4 million.

Using this analysis it was possible to approximate undermaintenance of the community's housing stock. It was estimated that $62.9 million was collected in rents while a total of $13.3 million was needed for property taxes and water and sewer charges; this left $49.5 million for operating and maintenance and return on capital. The assumption made at this point was that for the 51 percent of the buildings that were owner-occupied, a significant number of building owners would be willing to accept a slightly lower rate of return in order to put the extra funds into maintenance expenditures.[29] It was assumed that they were willing to accept a 7 percent, rather than an 8.5 percent, return.[30] A rate of return of 7 percent meant a total of $36.4 million for return on capital value. When this amount was deducted from the $49.5 million left from rents for operating and maintenance and return on capital, $13.1 million was left for expenditures on actual operating and maintenance items.

Housing undermaintenance (disinvestment) was therefore estimated to be:

$37.7 million = MBR requirement for operating maintenance
− $13.1 million = Amount estimated spent on operating and maintenance
$24.6 million = Undermaintenance of Bedford-Stuyvesant housing

It should be clearly noted that this method of estimating housing disinvestment makes the assumption that in Bedford-Stuyvesant the landlords' responses to situations where the amount of money needed for adequate operating and maintenance exceeds the rental receipts are to disinvestment through undermaintenance of properties. As was previously mentioned, it was assumed that the high rate of owner-occupancy would lead landlords to disinvest, but not to the maximum extent called for by a strict adherence to the maximum base rent versus rent receipts comparison.

Several other estimates were required to complete the income flow analysis of the housing sector.

Based on an analysis presented in Appendix C, it was estimated that average monthly mortgage payments on Bedford-Stuyvesant residential property were $170. Assuming this, and that 10 percent of the properties were owned free and clear, there were 9655 structures making $170 per month mortgage payments for a total yearly mortgage bill of $19.7 million.[31] Based on local and outside rates of building ownership it was estimated that local landlords paid $9.7 million, while outside landlords paid $10 million in mortgage payments. This was based on the 49-51 percent split of apartment ownership.

Deducting the total mortgage payments from the total return on capital value of $36.4 million left $16.7 million in profits. It was assumed that the profits were subjected to an average tax rate of 20 percent, which left after-tax profits of $13.4 million. These profits were distributed using the 49-51 percent split once again, with the result that local landlords received $6.6 million in after-tax profits, while outside landlords received $6.8 million.

The last calculation needed for the completion of the income flow statement that appears in a later section of this appendix was to estimate property taxes and water and sewer charges paid by local landlords. As 49 percent of the community's housing units were locally owned it was assumed that this percent of the total property, water, and sewer payments were paid by local landlords, or $5.5 million. In addition, it was found (see section 13) that 2.5 percent of the local business sales were in locally owned stores; therefore, 2.5 percent of the commercial property taxes and water and sewer charges, or $36,000 were paid by local residents. This gave a total payment of $5.5 million.

This had been a rather prolonged discussion of the estimates in the housing sector; but a necessary one since this is a critical sector and one in which very few estimates of disinvestment have been attempted. The procedures for Borough Park were the same as those for Bedford-Stuyvesant with a couple of significant exceptions. These exceptions will be noted and explained, but the rest of the discussion on housing estimates for the Borough Park community will be as brief as possible.

Borough Park

The 1970 Census found 68,918 housing units in Borough Park, of which 726 were either vacant, for sale, or for rent, leaving 68,192 occupied housing units. However, unlike Bedford-Stuyvesant, a significant number of these were one- and two-family dwellings; this was indicated by the *Multiple Dwelling Report* that found only 43,885 units in 4870 structures in Borough Park. From discussions with members of the housing section of the City Planning Commission it was estimated that 80 percent of those units not in multiple dwellings were probably in two-family homes, while the remaining 20 percent were single-family homes.

This meant that the housing stock of the community was composed of the following:

> 43,885 units in 4870 multiple dwellings
> 20,026 units in two-family homes
> 5,007 single-family homes

The average monthly contract rent per unit was $109, using the procedure previously described.

The number of rent-paying housing units was determined as follows:

> 68,918 = housing units
> −   726 = vacant, for sale, or for rent
> − 3,604 = owner-occupied units in multiple dwellings
> − 5,007 = owner-occupied single-family homes
> − 8,010 = owner-occupied units in two-family dwellings
> 51,571 housing units paying rent in 1969 in Borough Park

The 3,604 owner-occupied units in multiple dwellings was estimated from the analysis described in Appendix C, which indicated that 74 percent of the multiple dwelling structures in the community were owner-occupied. The 8,010 owner-occupied units in two-family homes was derived from an estimate that 80 percent of the 10,013 two-family homes were owner-occupied.

The total rent bill for the community was $67.5 million. But due to the significant number of housing units not in multiple dwellings, for purposes of MBR calculations (MBR only applies to multiple dwellings under rent control) an estimate of rents collected in multiple dwellings had to be made. Assuming all the vacancies were in multiple dwellings and correcting for the 3,604 owner-occupied units in such dwellings, left 39,555 rent paying units. This meant a rent bill of $51.7 million.

Of this amount, 68 percent ($35.2 million) was paid to local landlords while 32 percent ($16.5 million) was paid to outside landlords if the percents developed in the address match appearing in Appendix C are used.

The total amount paid in rent to local owners of multiple dwellings and two-family homes was estimated to be $50.9 million, while $16.5 million went to outside landlords.

The MBR estimates were derived just as before, using the following data:

> Residential property assessed at $251.8 million
> Property taxes of $8.7 million
> Water and sewer charges of $1.6 million

Operating and maintenance expenses of $22.9 million
(using 40 years for building age)
Return on capital value of $34.2 million

The total MBR was therefore $68.1 million. Undermaintenance was determined as follows:

$51.7 million in rent collected

−10.3 million for property taxes and water and sewer charges

$41.4 million for operating and maintenance and return

The assumption was then made that as there were even more owner-occupied buildings in Borough Park than in Bedford-Stuyvesant, and expectations about the area's future were excellent, owners would be willing to accept a 6 percent return and put the extra money into operating and maintenance expenditures. A 6 percent rate of return on capital value was calculated at $24.2 million. Subtracting this amount from $41.4 million left $17.3 million for operating and maintenance expenditures.

$22.9 million = MBR required for operating and maintenance

− $17.3 million = operating and maintenance expenditures

$ 5.6 million = undermaintenance

Thus, undermaintenance of the Borough Park multiple-dwelling housing stock was an estimated $5.6 million in 1969.

As in the case of Bedford-Stuyvesant, several other calculations had to be made for inclusion in the income flow statements that appear in later sections of this appendix.

It was assumed that 70 percent of the multiple-dwelling operating and maintenance expenditures were undertaken by local landlords and 30 percent by outside landlords. This split appeared entirely reasonable as the local-outside ownership for apartments was 68-32 percent. This meant local landlords spent $12.1 million, while outside landlords spent $5.2 million.

Mortgages on multiple dwellings were assumed to be $150 per month with 10 percent of the structures owned free and clear; therefore, mortgage payments were $7.9 million. These were split 68-32 so that local landlords paid $5.4 million, while outside landlords paid $2.5 million. Mortgages on one- and two-family homes were also assumed to be $150 per month so that single-family home mortgages were $9 million, while two-family mortgages were $18 million in annual payments. It was assumed that all single-family homes were owner-occupied or owned by local landlords. Therefore, total mortgage payments on all housing units by local landlords were $32.4 million, while comparable payments made by outside landlords were estimated at $2.5 million (outside landlords only made mortgage payments on 32 percent of the multiple dwellings).

To estimate operating and maintenance expenditures on one-family homes, the amount of $50 per month was used, while $75 per month was used for two-family homes; operating and maintenance costs came to $3 million and $9 million respectively for the two types of homes. Therefore, total operating and maintenance expenditures by local landlords were $24.1 million (single- and two-family structures plus their share of multiple dwellings), while outside landlords expended $5.2 million.

The last calculation in this sector was a determination of profits. By deducting mortgage costs for multiple dwelling units from the 6 percent return on capital value, a profit figure of $16.3 million was obtained. (The assumption was made of no profits on two-family homes.) After applying a 20 percent tax rate to these profits and distributing 68 percent to local landlords and 32 percent to outside landlords, the following after-tax profits were derived:

local landlords received $8.9 million in profits

outside landlords received S4.2 million in profits

A detailed listing of the types of multiple dwellings in each community is supplied in Table A-4.

13. Business Activity and Taxes

Bedford-Stuyvesant

The total sales of businesses located in Bedford-Stuyvesant were determined using Dun and Bradstreet computer tapes. While this source missed many of the very small establishments in the community, their sales dollars in relation to the community total were small, and the D&B estimate is probably a good one. Total gross sales were $345.2 million, and an analysis of the tapes revealed the following additional information:

Type of Establishment	Percent of All Establishments	Total Sales	Percent of Total Bedford-Stuyvesant Sales	Before Tax Profits
Corporations	54	$290,000,760	84	$23,200,061
Partnerships	12	27,619,120	8	2,761,912
Sole Proprietorships	32	27,619,120	8	2,761,912
		$345,239,000		$28,723,885

The figures for before-tax profits were based on an 8 percent rate of profit on gross sales for corporations, and a 10 percent rate of profit on gross sales for partnerships and sole proprietorships. From the author's observations, the 8 percent figure for corporations appeared to be a reasonable estimate for this community.

Frank Davis, in a recently published study of the Newark ghetto, estimated

Table A-4
Types of Multiple-Dwellings

Building Class	Number of Structures	Number of Units
Bedford-Stuyvesant		
Unclassified	55	243
Old-law tenement	3,425	18,975
New-law tenement	2,899	23,417
Old-law Single Room	8	7
New-law Single Room	4	12
Multiple dwelling: built after 1929	145	8,481
Converted before 1929 (class A)	1	13
Converted after 1929 (class B)	1,968	7,341
Apartment hotel built after 1929	1,427	5,535
Hotel-rooming house built after 1929	2	3
Hotel: built before 1929	3	*
Converted before 1929 (class B)	369	391
Converted after 1929 (class B)	422	445
	10,728	65,864
Borough Park		
Unclassified	5	12
Old-law tenement	65	258
New-law tenement	2,338	23,226
Multiple dwelling: built after 1929	208	12,840
Converted before 1929 (class A)	1	3
Converted after 1929 (class A)	1,511	4,650
Apartment hotel built before 1929	733	2,884
Hotel-rooming house: built after 1929	3	1
Converted before 1929 (class B)	2	5
Converted after 1929 (class B)	4	6
	4,870	43,885

*No report on number of units.

average net profit as a percent of gross sales at 4.1 percent.[32] However, considerations of the structure of the corporate sector in Bedford-Stuyvesant led the present author to use the 8 percent estimate in this study. It should be noted that the area of corporate profit margins in the ghetto is largely uncharted territory, as are so many other areas of urban poverty-area analysis.

One is on much firmer ground in using a 10 percent profit margin on gross sales for sole proprietorships, for several studies have been done on profit margins in these types of establishments. The Davis study found average net profits before taxes in several categories of retail and service establishments to be approximately 10 percent,[33] while a study by the Federal Trade Commission of low-income area retailers in the District of Columbia found net profits after taxes of 4.7 percent.[34] For the purposes of this study, however, the most important evidence used to make the 10 percent assumption was that furnished by a Columbia University study of the Harlem economy.[35] In a portion of the study entitled "The Profitability of Retail and Service Trades in Harlem and Bay Ridge,"[36] estimates of before-tax profits of 9.1 percent for Harlem and 10.6 percent for Bay Ridge were derived based on income tax return data.[37] These estimates helped to confirm the 10 percent before-tax profit assumption employed in this analysis. (Bay Ridge is an area of Brooklyn that is reasonably close to Borough Park in economic structure so that the 10 percent assumption can also be employed for Borough Park.)

Therefore, using the estimates of gross profits by type of establishment, combined with the appropriate tax rates, an estimate of after-tax profits was derived. The tax rates used were the following:[38]

New York City General Corporation Tax	6.7%
New York State General Corporation Tax	7.0%
Federal Corporate Income Tax (48% plus surcharge)	52.8%
New York City Unincorporated Business Tax	4.0%
New York State Unincorporated Business Tax	5.5%

Applying these tax rates to the corporate and unincorporated business income estimates gave the following estimated amounts of each tax paid by Bedford-Stuyvesant establishments:

New York City General Corporation Tax	$ 1,554,404
New York State General Corporation Tax	$ 1,624,004
Federal Corporate Income Tax	$10,571,433
New York City Unincorporated Business Tax	$ 208,801
New York State Unincorporated Business Tax	$ 303,810
Total business taxes	$14,262,452

Total before-tax profits were $28,723,885, with $14,461,433 left after taxes. These profits were distributed to local and nonlocal business owners using an address match of Bedford-Stuyvesant business owners names with their home addresses. This match showed that 2.5 percent of all sales dollars were accounted for by locally owned establishments, while the remainder were in local stores owned by people not living in the community. Local residents were allocated $361,536 in profits, while the remaining $14,099,897 in profits went to outsiders.

In addition to the business taxes previously estimated, all establishments in New York City paid a commercial rent tax equal to 7 percent of their rent payments. The payments of this tax were estimated in the following manner:

Collections for the calendar year 1969 of the commercial rent tax for the entire city were $87,312,893.[39]

Bedford-Stuyvesant sales were (according to the D&B tapes), 0.203 percent of New York City sales.

The Bedford-Stuyvesant contribution in commercial rent taxes was estimated at 0.203 percent of $87,312,893, or $177,245.

In addition to determining business sales, profits, and taxes it was necessary to estimate several other aspects of business activity for the income flow statements.

An estimate of the number of jobs in the community was needed in order to estimate business social security payments. Using the D&B tapes which listed the number of employees for most establishments, and adding the average number of workers per establishment for those listing no employment figures, an estimate of approximately 20,000 jobs was derived for the community. It is interesting to note that James Heilbrun's study of jobs in Harlem (an area with almost the same population as Bedford-Stuyvesant) estimated that there were 19,500 jobs in that community.[40] The further assumption was made that the jobs paid $95 per week;[41] therefore, the total wage bill was $98,800,000 for 1969. At the 4.8 percent social security rate paid by employers, this meant taxes for local establishments of $4,743,400.

In order to determine how many of these 20,000 local jobs were held by residents of the community it was necessary to estimate the percent of residents who worked in the community. Although the previously mentioned low-income study showed approximately 20 percent of the work force employed in the inner-city survey area,[42] a study of transportation in the Central Booklyn Model City area showed only 15 percent of resident work trips were to local destinations.[43] Due to the smaller size of Bedford-Stuyvesant in relation to the low-income survey area, this figure of 15 percent of the work force employed in the community was used. Based on the labor force participation rates found by Offner [155] for Bedford-Stuyvesant and the census figures on the age distribution of the population, it was possible to estimate that the community's labor force was approximately 67,000 workers. If 15 percent of these workers were employed in local jobs, then about 9,000 were employed in the community. This meant that 45 percent of the total wage bill paid by local firms was to local residents, or $44,460,000.

An estimate of business investment was based on a figure of 1.5 percent of gross sales. The Davis study of the Newark ghetto found that 1.3 percent of gross sales was used for investment,[44] so that a 1.5 percent figure for

Bedford-Stuyvesant is probably reasonable. This meant business investment of $5,178,585.

The Davis study of the Newark ghetto also showed that only 1.8 percent of the total ghetto gross sales dollars went back to black-owned firms, while 25.6 percent went to white-owned firms in the ghetto. He found that almost three-quarters of all gross sales dollars went directly out of the ghetto in returns to productive factors employed on the outside.[45] This phenomenon of sales dollars flowing right through the ghetto and out again had been expected; and a study of the Hough ghetto in Cleveland confirmed this view, as it found very slight linkages between ghetto firms.[46] The simplifying assumption was therefore made in this study that all factor payments (with the exception of wages to local residents) flowed directly to outsiders. Outside factor payments were estimated as follows:

$$
\begin{array}{ll}
\$345,239,000 & = \text{total sales} \\
-98,800,000 & = \text{wages} \\
-1,453,206 & = \text{property taxes and water and sewer charges} \\
-4,742,000 & = \text{social security payments} \\
-14,439,697 & = \text{business taxes} \\
-14,461,433 & = \text{profits} \\
\underline{-5,175,585} & = \text{investment} \\
\$206,164,679 & = \text{factor payments to outsiders}
\end{array}
$$

Borough Park

The procedure followed for Borough Park was the same as that for Bedford-Stuyvesant but using the following data:

Type of Establishment	Percent of All Establishments	Total Sales	Percent of Total Bedford-Stuyvesant Sales	Before Tax Profits
Corporations	45	$332,560,840	82	$26,604,867
Partnerships	11	20,278,100	5	2,027,810
Sole Proprietorships	44	52,723,060	13	5,272,306
		$405,562,000		$33,904,983

Business tax estimates were as follows:

New York City General Corporation Tax	$ 1,782,526
New York State General Corporation Tax	1,862,341
Federal Corporate Income Tax	12,122,880

New York City Unincorporated Business Tax		275,944
New York City Unincorporated Business Tax		401,506
Total business taxes		$15,867,747

Total before-tax profits were $33,904,983, with $18,037,236 left after taxes. The address match for Borough Park revealed that 23 percent of the sales dollars were contributed by locally owned establishments, while 77 percent were from outside-owned firms. After-tax profits were distributed using these percentages so that local owners received $4,148,564, and outside owners received $13,888,672.

Borough Park sales were 0.238 percent of total city sales so that the community's contribution in commercial rent payments was $207,805.

An estimate of 18,000 jobs was derived for Borough Park with 9,000 held by local residents. Weekly pay was estimated at $105 for a total wage bill of $98,280,000. Social security payments by employers was thus $4,717,440, and $49,140,000 in wages were paid by local employers to local residents.

Business investment (1.5 percent of gross sales) was $6,083,430.

Business factor payments were derived the same way as in the previous case and the assumption was again that all such payments left the community. Factor payments to outsiders were $256,486,170.

A complete listing of gross sales by two-digit SIC classification as taken from the Dun and Bradstreet tapes appears in Table A-5.

Table A-5
SIC Classification of Gross Sales (000)

SIC Number and Description	Bedford-Stuyvesant	Borough Park
15. Building construction, general contractors	$ 620	$ 2,534
17. Building construction, special contractors	6,351	6,676
20. Food and kindred products	16,250	14,010
22. Textile mill products	13,244	19,836
23. Apparel	18,287	19,699
24. Lumber and wood products	850	312
25. Furniture and fixtures	14,166	2,830
26. Paper and allied products	11,150	3,801
27. Printing and publishing	759	3,799
28. Chemicals	6,200	9,160
30. Rubber and misc. plastics	3,700	1,720
31. Leather products	10,124	2,645

Table A-5 (cont.)

SIC Number and Description	Bedford-Stuyvesant	Borough Park
32. Stone, clay, glass, and concrete products	512	3,480
33. Primary metal industries	350	1,100
34. Fabricated metal products	7,302	5,307
35. Machinery (not electrical)	21,970	4,296
36. Electrical machinery	3,074	23,100
37. Transportation equipment	1,194	0
38. Professional, scientific, and control instruments	410	3,137
39. Misc. manufacturing instruments	26,472	4,777
41. Local and suburban transit	10	15
42. Motor freight transportation and warehousing	2,051	1,710
47. Transportation services	200	0
49. Electric, gas, and sanitary services	0	67
50. Wholesale trade	82,021	103,833
52. Building materials, hardware	3,323	6,602
53. Retail trade, gen'l merchandise	2,516	34,295
54. Food stores	18,136	21,562
55. Automobile dealers	17,949	39,856
56. Apparel and accessory stores	6,789	11,547
57. Furniture, household furnishings, and equipment, etc.	7,729	11,286
58. Eating and drinking places	3,626	4,061
59. Misc. retail stores	14,224	27,054
65. Real estate	160	300
72. Personal services	17,537	2,478
73. Misc. business services	2,297	1,831
75. Automobile repair	3,054	2,343
76. Misc. repair	520	1,903
79. Amusement and recreation services	0	600
80. Medical and other health	2	2,000
Total	$345,239	$405,562

14. Personal and Property Taxes

Bedford-Stuyvesant

Social security payments by Bedford-Stuyvesant residents were taken to be 4.8 percent of adjusted gross income, or $13.6 million.

Federal personal income taxes were derived from *Statistics of Income, 1969*, published by the Internal Revenue Service which gave average income tax payments for separate adjusted gross income classes.[47] Total Federal income taxes paid by the community's residents were $30.9 million. A computer print-out, *New York State Personal Income Tax, 1969, All Taxable Returns*, in the offices of the New York City Finance Administration provided state income tax liabilities by income class which were used to compute this tax; such payments came to $5.8 million. Finance Administration tax liability schedules for the New York City personal income tax were used to compute the community's contribution of $960,000.

Total property taxes and water and sewer charges for Bedford-Stuyvesant were $15 million; however, a sample analysis of the *Final Tax Register* for Brooklyn revealed 1969 tax arrears of $3.3 million. Even though property owners were over $3 million in arrears they were still paying something on their back taxes, so an estimated $1.5 million in arrears was deducted from the assessed taxes and charges; as a result of this calculation, actual payments were taken to have been $13.5 million in 1969.

Borough Park

As has been the case in other sections of this appendix, the procedure followed for Borough Park was the same as for Bedford-Stuyvesant. Social security payments by residents were $29.5 million. Personal income taxes were as follows:

Federal	$81.8 million
State	$18.7 million
City	$ 3.3 million

Property taxes and water and sewer charges were $21.3 million with actual arrears estimated at $250,000; therefore, actual payments were approximately $21.1 million.

15. Consumer Expenditures and Taxes

Bedford-Stuyvesant

The assumption was made that 90 percent of local retail and service establishment sales were made to the residents of Bedford-Stuyvesant. Total local retail and service sales were $97.8 million; thus, about $88 million in sales were made to residents. Of the $97.8 million in total sales, $18.1 million was in food stores ($16.3 million to residents). Total resident consumption expenditures (derived as the residual in the *Sources and Uses of Funds* statement in section 16) were $214.1 million. As $88 million was spent in local stores, this left $126.1 million to be spent in outside stores by the community's residents.

Estimates of sales taxes were derived in the following manner: Sales taxes paid on local store consumption expenditures by residents (New York City sales tax = 3% and New York State sales tax = 3%) were taken as 90 percent of total retail and service sales by local establishments minus all food sales. New York City sales taxes were estimated as $1.5 million and New York State sales taxes were $1.5 million. Sales taxes paid by nonresidents on their nonfood purchases in local stores were $170,000 in city and $170,000 in state taxes.

One final sales tax estimate had to be derived based on expenditures by local residents at outside stores. The assumption was made that 25 percent of the total income of all the residents, or $100 million, was spent on food.[48] The residents spent $16.3 million locally on food; therefore, they had to spend $83.7 million nonlocally on food, all of which was not subject to a sales tax. From the total outside spending of $126.1 million, the outside food spending of $83.7 million had to be deducted, leaving $42.4 million to be spent in nonlocal stores on goods and services. The assumption that 80 percent of this spending was subject to the sales tax gave New York City sales tax payments of $1.3 million and New York State payments of $1.3 million for a total of $2.6 million.

The last items estimated were gasoline taxes and automobile registration and license fees. The Brooklyn Polytechnic Institute study of transportation needs in Bedford-Stuyvesant provided data for an estimate of 14,112 automobiles in Bedford-Stuyvesant.[49] It was assumed that each car had an average weight of 3000 pounds, so that total registration fees were $320,000 (a 3000-pound car paid $22.50). It was also assumed that 25,000 people had driver's licenses which cost them $3 per year each, for a total of $75,000. Each automobile was assumed to use five gallons of gasoline per week with a total tax per gallon of 11¢ (Federal = 4¢ and State = 7¢). Total gasoline taxes were $400,000, and the total of all taxes and fees together was $800,000.

Borough Park

For Borough Park the same procedure was followed for consumer expenditures and taxes. Local retail and service sales were $167.7 million with $150.9 million of this total sold to local residents. Of the $167.7 million in total sales, $21.6 million were in food stores (with $19.4 million to local residents). Total resident consumption expenditures were $391.2 million. As $150.9 million was spent locally, this left $240.3 million to be spent in outside stores by local residents.

Sales taxes paid on local store consumption expenditures by residents were $3.6 million in New York City sales taxes and $3.6 million in New York State sales taxes, for a total of $7.3 million. Sales taxes paid by nonresidents for their nonfood purchases at local stores were $400,000 in city and $400,000 in state sales taxes, for a total of $800,000.

Borough Park residents spent $180 million on food. They spent $19.4 million on food locally; therefore, they spent $160.6 million nonlocally on food, all of which was not subject to a sales tax. Of the total resident spending of $240.3 million, the outside food spending of $160.6 million was deducted, leaving $79.7 million for outside nonfood spending by the community's residents. Assuming that 80 percent was subject to a sales tax meant that $2.4 million was paid in New York City sales taxes and another $2.4 million in New York State taxes, for a total of $4.8 million.

Gasoline taxes and automobile license and registration fees were calculated in a different way than for Bedford-Stuyvesant. A comparison of 1960 Census data for the two communities for "private auto or carpool" use by residents revealed that 1.5 times as many Borough Park residents used automobiles. Therefore, the 14,112 automobile estimate for Bedford-Stuyvesant was multiplied by a factor of 1.5 to get 21,168 automobiles in Borough Park; licenses were also multiplied by 1.5 to arrive at a total for Borough Park of 37,500. Using the same cost figures and gasoline use assumptions for Borough Park gave the following estimates: $500,000 in registration fees, $100,000 in license fees, and $600,000 in gasoline taxes, for a total of $1.2 million.

16. Sources and Uses of Funds by Residents

Table A-6 summarizes, from the preceding sections of this appendix, the statements of sources and uses of funds by residents of each community in 1969.

17. Income Flows

Tables A-7 and A-8 summarize statements of inflows and outflows of income for the two communities, as derived from this appendix.

Table A-6
Sources and Uses of Funds by Residents

	Bedford-Stuyvesant	Borough Park
Sources of Purchasing Power		
Adjusted gross income	$282,782,000	$615,389,000
Social Security	21,246,664	84,363,324
Unemployment Compensation	8,023,808	4,011,904
Workmen's Compensation	4,452,474	8,904,948
Public assistance	87,954,050	10,906,164
Subtotal	404,458,996	723,575,340
Consumer credit extended	17,611,273	28,178,037
Policy winnings	11,694,774	–
Total purchasing power (sources)	433,765,043	751,753,377
Uses of Purchasing Power		
Taxes:		
Personal income taxes	37,689,263	103,856,989
Individual Social Security taxes	13,782,000	29,538,672
Property taxes and water and sewer charges paid by residents	5,547,603	12,149,748
Subtotal	57,018,866	145,543,409
Savings	20,222,950	65,121,781
Consumer credit repaid	16,186,832	25,898,931
Subtotal	93,428,648	236,564,121
Rent Payments	62,852,736	67,454,868
Mortgage payments by resident owners	9,651,138	32,400,792
Operating and maintenance expenditures by resident owners	7,000,000	24,101,630
Subtotal	171,932,522	360,521,411
Policy played	16,706,820	–
Narcotics	30,978,886	–
Subtotal	219,618,228	
Other consumer expenditures (residual, including taxes)	214,146,815	391,231,966
Total purchasing power (uses)	$433,765,043	$751,753,377

Table A-7
Inflows of Income

Income	Bedford-Stuyvesant			Borough Park
Adjusted gross income	$282,782,000			$615,389,000
Profits from local businesses received by resident owners $361,536		$ 4,148,564		
Profits from local multiple dwellings received by resident owners $6,563,079			8,855,558	
Wages paid by local firms to local residents $44,460,000			49,140,000	
Social Security	21,246,664			84,363,324
Unemployment Compensation	8,023,808			4,011,904
Workmen's Compensation	4,452,474			8,904,948
Public assistance	87,954,050			10,906,164
Consumer credit extensions	17,611,273			28,178,037
Policy winnings	11,694,774			
Government services	166,531,641			82,677,503
Sales by local retail and service establishments to nonresidents	9,781,200			16,771,800
Sales by local corporations to nonresidents	237,427,000			237,844,000
Business investment	5,178,585			6,083,430
Total inflows of income	$852,683,469			$1,095,130,110

Table A-8
Outflows of Income

Income	Bedford-Stuyvesant	Borough Park
Personal taxes:		
Individual income taxes	$ 37,689,263	$103,856,989
Individual Social Security taxes	13,782,000	29,538,672
Housing:		
Property taxes and water and sewer charges paid by residents	5,547,603	12,149,748
Mortgage payments by residents owners	9,651,138	32,400,792
Operating and maintenance expenditures by resident owners	7,000,000	24,101,630
Rental payments to outside owners	32,054,895	16,556,141
Profits to outside owners	(6,830,960)	(4,167,322)
Housing disinvestment	24,624,682	5,633,426
Vacant building loss	1,181,500	288,800
Business:		
Business taxes	14,439,697	16,075,552
Business Social Security payments	4,742,400	4,717,440
Business property taxes and water sewer charges	1,453,206	5,882,172
Wages paid to nonresidents	54,340,000	49,140,000
Factor payments to outsiders	206,164,679	256,486,170
Profits to outside owners	14,099,097	13,888,672
Consumption:		
Consumption expenditures by residents in outside businesses	126,855,958	240,285,766
NYC sales taxes	(1,273,152)	(2,390,747)
NYS sales taxes	(1,273,152)	(2,390,747)
Sales Taxes paid by residents on local consumption expenditures		
NYC sales taxes	1,516,158	3,636,927
NYS sales taxes	1,516,158	3,636,927
Sales taxes paid by nonresidents at local businesses		
NYC sales taxes	168,480	404,103
NYS sales taxes	168,480	404,103
Savings	20,222,950	65,121,781
Repayments of consumer credit	16,186,832	25,808,931
Policy played	16,706,820	–
Narcotics	30,978,886	–
Total outflows of income	$640,351,739	$910,094,742

Notes

1. In 1969, the New York City Planning Commission's PLAN FOR NEW YORK CITY [147] was published in six volumes. While one may take exception to some of its recommendations, these volumes present the clearest and most current statistical information and detailed maps available for New York City and its component communities.

2. Ibid., vol. 3, pp. 39-46.

3. Ibid., vol. 3, pp. 129-136.

4. Dual Labs, "Zip Area Income Data-Zip Aid: Detailed Explanation of Terms," (1970), pp. 7, 8. The definition of adjusted gross income includes wages and salaries minus such items as operating business expenses, moving expenses, education deductions for various items, losses on capital assets, etc.

5. New York City Department of Health, Bureau of Health Statistics and Analysis, VITAL STATISTICS BY HEALTH AREA AND HEALTH CENTER DISTRICTS, 1969, p. 43.

6. U.S. Department of Commerce [204], p. 10.

7. Conference Board [45], p. 109.

8. Ibid., p. 111.

9. Galenson [72], p. 213.

10. U.S. Department of Labor [204], p. 193.

11. U.S. Department of Labor, Bureau of Labor Statistics, Black Americans, Washington, D.C.: Government Printing Office, 1971, p. 20.

12. U.S. Department of Labor [204], p. 193.

13. Ibid.

14. Lasswell, McKenna, and Manoni [115].

15. New York City, EXECUTIVE BUDGET 1969-1970, pp. 156-167.

16. New York City, EXECUTIVE BUDGET, 1969-1970, p. 320.

17. Meyer and Lansky [135].

18. Burnham [32].

19. Housing and Development Administration (HDA) [99].

20. Ibid., p. 21.

21. Environmental Protection Administration [61].

22. HDA [99], p. 50.

23. Ibid., p. 23.

24. Ibid., p. 125.

25. Ibid., p. 21.

26. Ibid., p. 27.

27. Sternlieb's study of rent-controlled housing in NYC found great variations in assessment to market value ratios depending on numerous factors, with ratios on one, two, and three family homes at 50%, and walk-up structures at 60-70% of actual sales values. See Sternlieb [192], p. 263.

28. HDA [99], p. 30.

29. Sternlieb [191], p. 174. Sternlieb found that owner-occupied structures were better maintained.

30. The question of rates of return on ghetto rental properties is still very much an open one. Sternlieb [191], found, for a sample of 32 parcels owned by a single tenement management company in Newark, rates of return on total property value of around 10-12%. In a later study of the NYC rent-controlled housing stock he found a large number of types of rent-controlled structures yielding returns of less than 6%; see Sternlieb [192], p. 292. Another study, in Wisconsin, based on 52 owners of 47 parcels in Milwaukee's slum areas, showed an average rate of return on owner's invested capital of over 25% in over 20% of the cases; see Sporn [188], p. 338.

31. This finding that mortgage payments were about 30% of gross rentals is supported by Sternlieb's findings for the NYC rental housing market that over one-fourth of each group of buildings in his study had debt service of at least 23%, and 10% had debt service of over 35% of rentals received. Due to the traditional problems in securing reasonable mortgages in the ghetto, the figure derived for Bedford-Stuyvesant appears entirely reasonable; see Sternlieb [192], p. 252.

32. Davis [51], p. 49.

33. Ibid., p. 47.

34. Federal Trade Commission [64], p. 106.

35. Columbia University Development Planning Workshop [44].

36. Ibid., vol. 2, pp. 285-326.

37. Ibid., p. 286.

38. Commerce Clearinghouse, 1971 GUIDEBOOK TO NEW YORK TAXES, 1971.

39. ANNUAL REPORT OF THE COMPTROLLER OF THE CITY OF NEW YORK, fiscal year 1969-1970, p. 175.

40. Columbia University [44], vol. 1, p. 38.

41. U.S. Department of Commerce [204], p. 4.

42. Ibid., p. 12.

43. Polytechnic Institute of Brooklyn [165], p. 141.

44. Davis [51], p. 66.

45. Ibid., p. 67.

46. Oakland, Sparrow, and Stettler [150], p. 175.

47. Internal Revenue Service, STATISTICS OF INCOME, 1969, INDIVIDUAL INCOME TAX RETURNS, Table 1-1.

48. Oakland, Sparrow, and Stettler [150], p. 168.

49. Polytechnic Institute [165], p. 35.

Appendix B
Historical Income and
Population Estimates

On the basis of decennial census data, the estimates shown in Table B-1 were made for the two communities:

Table B-1
Population and Income Estimates Based on Decennial Census Data

Bedford-Stuyvesant

Year	Population	Negro	% Negro
1970	218,829	177,094	81
1960	227,627	163,600	72
1950	246,384	124,482	51
1940	233,551	56,282	24
1930	231,212	25,616	11
1920	252,559	9,221	4

Borough Park

Year	Population	Negro	% Negro
1970	185,533	1,030	.6
1960	199,925	683	.3
1950	222,257	507	.2
1940	220,626	763	.3
1930	202,144	382	.2
1920	94,706	255	.3

Bedford Stuyvesant

Year	Income (Current $)	Income (Constant $)	% Increase
1969[a]	$404,458,996	$404,458,996[b]	30.3
1959	242,742,589	310,467,771	4.7
1949	201,336,930	296,196,624	

Borough Park

Year	Income (Current $)	Income (Constant $)	% Increase
1969	$723,575,340	$723,575,340	52.2

Table B-1 (cont.)

	Borough Park (cont.)		
Year	*Income (Current $)*	*Income (Constant $)*	*% Increase*
1959	371,734,645	475,448,611	30.1
1949	248,254,030	365,181,678	

	Central Brooklyn Low-Income Area		
Year [c]	*Income (Current $)*	*Income (Constant $)*	*% Increase*
1969	$841,052,500	$841,952,500	3.4
1959	635,591,597	812,921,048	10.4
1949	498,337,930	733,055,095	

[a]The 1969 income estimates for Bedford-Stuyvesant and Borough Park are based on estimates described in Appendix A.

[b]Current dollar amounts converted to constant 1969 dollars using the Consumer Price Index for the New York Metropolitan Region as presented in The Conference Board, A GUIDE TO CONSUMER MARKETS: 1970 (New York: Conference Board, 1970), p. 197.

[c]Author's estimates computed from U.S. Department of Commerce, Bureau of the Census, EMPLOYMENT PROFILES OF SELECTED LOW-INCOME AREA, BROOKLYN BOROUGH, NEW YORK CITY—AREA 2 (Washington, D.C.: Government Printing Office, January 1972), Table I: Total Family Income for Civilian Noninstitutional Population, p. 8.

Public assistance payments, in the low-income area of Central Brooklyn were $203,892,750 in 1969 by the author's estimate. Thus, public assistance payments in this ghetto of almost 500,000 people amounted to close to one-quarter of total income.

It is instructive to subtract public assistance payments from the 1959 and 1969 income estimates for Bedford-Stuyvesant and then compare changes in total income over the decade.

$$\begin{array}{ll} \$404,458,996 & = 1969 \text{ total income} \\ -\ 87,954,050 & = 1969 \text{ public assistance} \\ \hline \$316,504,946 & \end{array}$$

If it is assumed that Bedford-Stuyvesant received the same percent of the total New York City public assistance budget in 1959 as it did in 1969 (7.613%), then public assistance payments in 1959 were $17,292,855; in 1969 dollars these payments would be $22,117,561.[1]

When the 1959 public assistance payments are deducted from total 1959 income for Bedford-Stuyvesant (in 1969 dollars), a non-public-assistance income for the community in 1959 is left amounting to $288,350,210. When public assistance payments are deducted from the decade's increased income in

Bedford-Stuyvesant, the increase in constant dollars in non-public-assistance income is 9.7 percent—quite a drop from the original income increase of 30.3 percent. This is not hard to understand, as the average monthly public assistance caseload for the entire city increased from 50,000 in 1959 to 400,000 in 1969.[2]

A last point concerning the entire Central Brooklyn low-income survey area should be noted. When one observes that real income in this ghetto increased only 3.4 percent from 1959 to 1969, it is highly probable that when the increased public assistance payments are deducted, the real earnings of the residents in our nation's largest urban ghetto actually decreased over the last decade.

Notes

1. Figures taken from New York City BUDGET FISCAL YEAR 1959-60, p. 1081.

2. Figures taken from ibid., and the New York City EXECUTIVE BUDGET FISCAL YEAR 1969-70, p. 194.

Appendix C
Homeowner Analysis

1. Multiple Dwelling and Owner Address Match

Computer print-outs from the Housing and Development Administration's *Multiple Dwelling File* were obtained and used in this match along with HDA's *Telephone Master List* giving the owner's home address for every multiple dwelling in New York City. Every third building in the multiple-dwelling listing was matched with its owner (over 3500 matches in Bedford-Stuyvesant and over 1600 in Borough Park) to determine whether the building was owner-occupied, owned by a resident living in another building in the community, or owned by someone residing outside of the community. The results of this effort appear in Table C-1.

Table C-1
Resident Location of Multiple-Dwelling Owners

Owner Location	Percent of All Multiple Dwellings	Percent of All Apartments in Multiple Dwellings
Bedford-Stuyvesant:		
Occupant	51%	32%
Lives in community	19	17
Lives outside community	30	51
Borough Park:		
Occupant	74	50
Lives in community	14	18
Lives outside community	12	32

As can be seen, 51 percent of the multiple dwelling structures are owner-occupied, but only 32 percent of the apartments in the community are in buildings that are owner-occupied.

In Borough Park the incidence of owner-occupied multiple dwellings and apartments in owner-occupied structures is significantly greater than in Bedford-Stuyvesant.

The results for Bedford-Stuyvesant show that in relation to other ghetto areas, the rate of owner-occupancy is high. Sternblieb's sample of Newark ghetto property revealed that 36.6 percent of the parcels were owner-occupied, and an additional 10.2 percent were owned by people living in the study area.[1] Michael Zweig's study of ownership in central Harlem found (using a 25 percent sample of city blocks) that 49 percent of the parcels (but only 16.5 percent of the assessed value) were owned by Harlem residents. Zweig used records from the Department of Real Estate that tended to overstate the incidence of local ownership, as he found one-third of the parcels held in corporate form and assigned all of these parcels to Harlem owners. Also contributing to the overstatement was the fact that address changes by property owners after they acquired a parcel were not recorded in Zweig's data source. Therefore, the higher incidence of corporate ownership and the inability to determine owner address changes tended to overstate the local ownership rate by a not insignificant amount.[2]

The present author's match was done with up-to-date telephone listings currently in use in the emergency repair program at HDA and therefore avoided the problem of owner address changes. The author found only a small incidence of corporate ownership in Bedford-Stuyvesant.

2. The Bedford-Stuyvesant Homeowner

The Bedford-Stuyvesant Restoration Corporation has been operating a mortgage pool since 1968. This pool helps residents refinance existing mortgages and make new purchases of homes in the community on reasonable financial terms. This study was based on a sample of 106 one- to four-family homes that were refinanced by their owners during 1969. The information in the files on each property was extensive and provided a rich source of data on homeowners in the area. Table C-2 presents a summary of the results of this study.

The average FHA estimate of home market value was $20,079. The properties had average mortgages of the following amounts on them:

first mortgages	$10,325
second mortgages	$ 7,375
third mortgages	$ 5,350

The above figures are the average initial amounts listed for the various types of mortgages.

An interesting feature of the Bedford-Stuyvesant homeowners is the large number of families with both husband and wife working, as can be seen from Table C-2.

The mortgage pool provides FHA-insured 25- to 30-year mortgages at reasonable interest rates, thus greatly reducing the monthly payments of the homeowners. Of the 106 properties, 70 had two mortgages (6 had three mortgages), and for these 70 properties the average monthly mortgage payments were $170 before entering the pool and $118 after refinancing. The refinanced homeowners were able to save approximately 30 percent on their monthly

Table C-2
Summary of Data on 106 Bedford-Stuyvesant Homeowners

Total Assets:		Total Liabilities:	
Cash in bank	$ 120,921	Personal loans	$ 25,300
Auto value	76,100	Auto loans	30,500
Cash surrender value		Home improvement loans	104,950
of life insurance	18,850	Other loans	11,300
Household furnishings	175,500	Total	$172,050
Stocks and Bonds	23,000		
Home Equity[a]	1,275,048		
Total	$1,789,419		

Average Monthly Housing Expenses:		Net Wealth:	
Mortgage	$135	Total	$1,617,369
Fire insurance	7	Average	15,258
Taxes	38	Family income:	
Maintenance	18	Total	1,275,010[b]
Heat and utilities	47	Average	12,028
Total	$245		

Status of Homeowners:	Number
Retired	1
Divorced, separated, or widowed	20
Single	5
Only husband working	22
Both husband and wife working	58

[a]Home equity defined as the FHA estimated market value of the property minus any outstanding mortgage balances.
[b]Of this total family income, $195,600 was from apartment rentals; 84 of the 106 families rented at least one apartment in their home.

mortgage payments, and thereby obtained much needed money for home improvements. In fact, it is an FHA requirement that all refinanced homes put at least 10 percent of the value of the home into repairs and improvements.

An interesting picture developed as to the identity of the prepool mortgage lenders in the area, and the results are presented in Table C-3.

Eleven properties were refinanced when they were free and clear. Of the 95 mortgaged buildings, 70 had 2nd mortgages and 6 had 3rd mortgages. It is interesting to note that 70 of the 171 mortgages (41 percent) were placed with private individuals prior to refinancing.

Table C-3

Number of Mortgages Held by Mortgage Lenders in Bedford-Stuyvesant

Mortgage Lender	1st Mortgage	2nd Mortgage	3rd Mortgage	Total
Private	20	45	5	70
Brevoort	15			15
Lawrence-Cederhurst	9			9
State Funding Corporation	8			8
Peerless Realty		8		8
East Brooklyn	6			6
Carver	7			7
Freedom	3	1		4
Woodside	5			5
Allied Federal	2			2
Washington Heights	2			2
United Mutual Insurance	1		1	2
Broadway Realty		1		1
Knickerbocker Realty	1			1
Cardinal Realty		2		2
3-G Realty		1		1
Flatbush Federal	1			1
Central Federal	1			1
Roosevelt	1			1
Ebenezer Baptist Church	1			1
First National City		2		2
Paragon Progressive		1		1
Woodmere Investors		1		1
Eastern Service Corporation	3			3
Atlantic	2			2
Dime	1			1
Greenpoint		1		1
Atlas		1		1
Metropolitan		1		1
All State Investors		1		1
Carold Corporation		1		1
City Federal	1			1
Gamble Realty		2		2
Hamilton	1			1
Manufacturers Hanover	2	1		3
Citation Corporation	2			2
Totals	95	70	6	171

And finally, the FHA estimate of the market value of each property was compared with its assessed value to determine the average assessed value to market value ratio for the sample. The average ratio was 40 percent with a standard deviation of 9 percent. The assessed-value: market-value ratio is presented below:

Ratio	No. of Parcels
15-19%	1
20-24	0
25-29	5
30-34	30
35-39	19
40-44	20
45-49	14
50-54	11
55-59	2
60-64	4
	106

Notes

1. Sternlieb [191], p. 131.
2. Zweig [220], pp. 24-26.

Appendix D
Vacant Building and
Lot Survey

In November 1969, the Sanborn Map Company inspected the Bedford-Stuyvesant area; and under a special arrangement with the City of New York, recorded the addresses of all vacant buildings in the area. By abstracting information from their fire insurance field atlases the company was able to further determine if the building was first observed vacant in 1969. In doing this vacant-structure inventory, the Sanborn field worker found 409 completely vacant buildings in Bedford-Stuyvesant, including 142 that were first observed vacant in 1969. The total assessed value of these 142 structures was determined by the author to be $1,181,500.

In March and April of 1970 the company field worker surveyed Borough Park and found 34 completely vacant structures, including 15 that were first observed vacant in 1969. These 15 buildings had an assessed value of $288,800.

This author wanted to determine how many completely vacant buildings and vacant lots currently existed in Bedford-Stuyvesant, so in March 1972, he conducted his own field survey. Every property in the area was viewed, and when a building or a lot was found vacant it was recorded on a map of the area drafted for the Community Renewal Program by the City Planning Commission showing each building at a scale of one inch equals 200 feet. The field survey revealed 566 vacant buildings and 780 vacant lots, excluding public housing in construction and lots currently being cleared for public housing. Thus, in the 28 months between the Sanborn survey and the author's survey, an estimated 155 totally vacant buildings appeared; that is an average of over 67 additional vacant buildings per year from November 1969 to March 1972. The true vacant-building figure is higher than this, as buildings that were vacant at the time of the 1969 survey may appear as vacant lots in the 1972 survey, or as areas where public housing is presently being constructed.

Bibliography

Bibliography

1. Abrams, Charles. FORBIDDEN NEIGHBORS. New York: Harper & Brothers, 1955.
2. Ackerman, Bruce. "Regulating Slum Housing Markets on Behalf of the Poor: Of Housing Codes, Housing Subsidies, and Income Redistribution Policy." YALE LAW JOURNAL 80 (May 1971), 1093-1197.
3. Allen, Louis L. "Making Capitalism Work in the Ghettos." HARVARD BUSINESS REVIEW (May-June 1969), 83-92.
4. Allen, Robert L. BLACK AWAKENING IN CAPITALIST AMERICA, Garden City, N.Y.: Doubleday, 1970.
5. Allvine, Fred C. "Black Business Development." JOURNAL OF MARKETING 34 (April 1970), 1-7.
6. America, Richard F. "What Do You People Want?" HARVARD BUSINESS REVIEW (March-April 1969), 103-112.
7. Archibald, G.C. "Regional Multiplier Effects in the U.K." OXFORD ECONOMIC PAPERS 19 (March 1967), 22-45.
8. Ashenfelter, Orley. "Changes in Labor Market Discrimination Over Time." JOURNAL OF HUMAN RESOURCES 5 (Fall 1970), 403-430.
9. Ballon, Herbert J. BROOKLYN NEIGHBORHOODS. New York: Brooklyn Council for Social Planning, June 1941.
10. Balogh, T. "The Mechanism of Neo-Imperialism." In K.W. Rothschild, editor. POWER IN ECONOMICS. Baltimore: Penguin, 1971. Pp. 319-340.
11. Baron, Harold M. "Black Powerlessness in Chicago." TRANSACTION 6 (November 1968), 27-33.
12. Baron, Harold M. "Race and Status in School Spending: Chicago, 1961-1966." JOURNAL OF HUMAN RESOURCES 6 (Winter 1971), 3-24.
13. Baron, Harold M. "The Web of Urban Racism." In Louis L. Knowles and Kenneth Prewitt, editors. INSTITUTIONAL RACISM IN AMERICA. Englewood Cliffs, N.J.: Prentice-Hall, 1969. Pp. 134-176.
14. Bateman, Worth, and Harold M. Hochman. "Social Problems and the Urban Crisis: Can Public Policy Make a Difference?" AMERICAN ECONOMIC REVIEW 61 (May 1971), 346-353.
15. Bator, Francis M. "The Anatomy of Market Failure." QUARTERLY JOURNAL OF ECONOMICS 72 (August 1958), 351-379.
16. Baumol, William J. "External Economies and Second-Order Optimality Conditions." AMERICAN ECONOMIC REVIEW 59, pt. I (June 1964).
17. Baumol, William J. "Macroeconomics of Unbalanced Growth: The Anatomy of Urban Crisis." AMERICAN ECONOMIC REVIEW 62 (June 1967), 415-426.
18. Baumol, William J. WELFARE ECONOMICS AND THE THEORY OF THE STATE. Cambridge, Mass.: Harvard University Press, 1969.

19. Becker, Gary S. THE ECONOMICS OF DISCRIMINATION. 2nd ed. Chicago: University of Chicago Press, 1971.

20. Bedford-Stuyvesant Restoration Corporation. BUILDING A NEW BEDFORD-STUYVESANT. New York: the Corporation, 1971.

21. Bedford-Stuyvesant Restoration Corporation. A GUIDE TO BEDFORD-STUYVESANT. New York: the Corporation, 1972.

22. Bergmann, Barbara R. "The Effect on White Incomes of Discrimination in Employment." JOURNAL OF POLITICAL ECONOMY 79 (March-April 1971), 294-313.

23. Bergsman, Joel. "Alternatives to the Non-Gilded Ghetto." PUBLIC POLICY 19 (Spring 1971), 309-322.

24. Blackman, Courtney N. "An Eclectic Approach to the Problem of Black Economic Development." THE REVIEW OF BLACK POLITICAL ECONOMY 2 (Fall 1971), 3-27.

25. Blauner, Robert. "Internal Colonialism and Ghetto Revolt." SOCIAL PROBLEMS 16 (Spring 1970), 393-406.

26. Bluestone, Barry. "The Political Economy of Black Capitalism." In David M. Gordon, editor. PROBLEMS IN POLITICAL ECONOMY; AN URBAN PERSPECTIVE. Lexington, Mass.: D.C. Heath, 1971. Pp. 138-146.

27. Boggs, James. "The Myth and Irrationality of Black Capitalism." THE REVIEW OF BLACK POLITICAL ECONOMY 1 (Spring-Summer 1970), 14-35.

28. Brimmer, Andrew F., and Henry S. Terrell. "The Economic Potential of Black Capitalism." Mimeo., for American Economic Association meetings, December 1969.

29. Brooklyn Church and Mission Federation. SURVEY OF BEDFORD-STUYVESANT AREA. New York, Spring 1938.

30. Browne, Robert S. "Cash Flows in a Ghetto Community." REVIEW OF BLACK POLITICAL ECONOMY 1 (Winter-Spring 1971), 28-39.

31. Burks, Edward C. "Growth of Poverty in City Creating New Poor Zones." NEW YORK TIMES. April 10, 1972. Pp. 1, 40.

32. Burnham, David. "Police Efficiency Constant All Over City, Study Finds." NEW YORK TIMES, February 15, 1972, p. 22.

33. Burnham, David, "A Wide Disparity is Found in Crime Throughout City," NEW YORK TIMES. February 14, 1972, pp. 1, 16.

34. Cain, Glen G., and Harold W. Watts. "Problems in Making Policy Inferences from the Coleman Report." Discussion Paper #28-68. Madison: Institute for Research on Poverty, University of Wisconsin, 1968.

35. Cairnes, J.E. SOME LEADING PRINCIPLES OF POLITICAL ECONOMY NEWLY EXPOUNDED. London: Macmillan, 1887.

36. Caplovitz, David, THE POOR PAY MORE. New York: Free Press, 1967.

37. Carmichael, Stokely, and Charles V. Hamilton. BLACK POWER. New York: Random House, 1967.

38. Case, Fred C. "Housing the Underhoused in the Inner City." JOURNAL OF FINANCE 26 (May 1971), 427-444.

39. Fred C. Case, Claude Elias, Jr., William Hippaka, Sylvia Lane, and Wallace F. Smith. HOUSING THE UNDERHOUSED: THE CALIFORNIA STUDIES. Housing, Real Estate, and Urban Land Studies Program. Los Angeles: University of California at Los Angeles, May 1971.

40. Center for Community Change and National Urban League. NATIONAL SURVEY OF HOUSING ABANDONMENT. Chicago, April 1971.

41. Chipman, John S. THE THEORY OF INTER-SECTORAL MONEY FLOWS AND INCOME FORMATION. Baltimore: Johns Hopkins University Press, 1951.

42. City of New York. EXECUTIVE BUDGET FOR 1969-1970. New York: 1969.

43. Coase, R.H. "The Problem of Social Cost." JOURNAL OF LAW AND ECONOMICS 3 (October 1960), 1-44.

44. Columbia University Development Planning Workshop. THE ECONOMY OF HARLEM. 2 vols. New York: Columbia University, 1968 and 1969. Mimeo.

45. Conference Board. A GUIDE TO CONSUMER MARKETS 1970. New York, 1970.

46. Cook, Fred C. "The Black Mafia Moves into the Numbers Racket." NEW YORK TIMES, April 4, 1971, pp. 26-27, 107-112.

47. Cox, William E. "A Commercial Structure Model for Depressed Neighborhoods." JOURNAL OF MARKETING 33 (July 1969), 1-9.

48. Cross, Theodore L. BLACK CAPITALISM. New York: Atheneum, 1969.

49. Daniels, Mark. "An Analytical Perspective on the Economics of Black Capitalism." Inter-University Committee on Urban Economics PROCEEDINGS, September 11-12, 1969. Mimeo.

50. Darwent, David. "Externality, Agglomeration Economies, and City Size." Working Paper #109, Berkely, Cal.: Institute of Urban and Regional Development, University of California, January 1970.

51. Davis, Frank G. THE ECONOMICS OF BLACK COMMUNITY DEVELOPMENT. Chicago: Markham, 1972.

52. Davis, Morton D. GAME THEORY. New York: Basic Books, 1970.

53. Davis, Otto A., and Andrew B. Whinston. "Economics of Urban Renewal." LAW AND CONTEMPORARY PROBLEMS 26 (Winter 1961), 105-117.

54. DEFAULTS ON FHA-INSURED MORTGAGES (DETROIT). Hearings before a Subcommittee of the Committee on Government Operations, House of Representatives, 92 Congress, 1 Session, December 2-4, 1971.

55. Doctors, Samuel I., and Sharon Lockwood. "Opportunity Funding Corporation: An Analysis." LAW AND CONTEMPORARY PROBLEMS 36 (Spring 1971), 227-237.

56. Dos Santos, Theotonic. "The Structure of Dependence." AMERICAN ECONOMIC REVIEW 60 (May 1970), 231-236.

57. Downs, Anthony. URBAN PROBLEMS AND PROSPECTS. Chicago: Markham, 1970.

58. Drake, St. Clair, and Horace P. Cayton. BLACK METROPOLIS: A STUDY OF NEGRO LIFE IN A NORTHERN CITY, rev. ed., 2 vols. New York: Harper & Row, 1962.

59. EBS Management Consultants, Inc. INITIAL EVALUATION OF THE BEDFORD-STUYVESANT SPECIAL IMPACT PROGRAM. Washington, D.C., June 30, 1969.

60. Edel, Matthew. "Development or Dispersal?: Approaches to Ghetto Poverty." Working Paper #1. Cambridge: Center for Community Economic Development, March 1970. Mimeo.

61. Environmental Protection Administration. AMENDMENTS TO RULES AND REGULATIONS FIXING UNIFORM ANNUAL CHARGES AND EXTRA AND MISCELLANEOUS CHARGES FOR THE SUPPLY OF WATER, AND RULES AND REGULATIONS RELATING TO SEWER RENTS. New York: June 30, 1970.

62. Farr, Walter, Lance Liebman, and Jeffrey S. Wood, DECENTRALIZING CITY GOVERNMENT. New York: The Bar Association of the City of New York, 1972. Draft copy.

63. Faux, Geoffrey. CDCs: NEW HOPE FOR THE INNER CITY. New York: Twentieth Century Fund, 1971.

64. Federal Trade Commission. "Economic Report on Installment Credit and Retail Sales Practices of District of Columbia Retailers." In Frederick Sturdivant, editor. THE GHETTO MARKETPLACE. New York: Free Press, 1969, 76-107.

65. Ferretti, Fred. "Patterson Charges U.S. Census Shorts City on Aid Funds." NEW YORK TIMES. March 4, 1972, p. 29.

66. Flint, Jerry M. "Inner-City Decay Causes Business Life to Wither." NEW YORK TIMES. July 19, 1971, pp. 1, 29.

67. Forman, Robert E. BLACK GHETTOS, WHITE GHETTOS, AND SLUMS. Englewood Cliffs, N.J.: Prentice-Hall, 1971.

68. Frank, Andre Gunder. CAPITALISM AND UNDERDEVELOPMENT IN LATIN AMERICA. New York: Monthly Review Press, 1969.

69. Friedly, Philip. "A Note on the Retail Trade Multiplier and Residential Mobility." JOURNAL OF REGIONAL SCIENCE 6 (Summer 1965), 57-63.

70. Fusfeld, Daniel R. "The Basic Economics of the Urban and Racial Crisis." REVIEW OF BLACK POLITICAL ECONOMY 1 (Spring-Summer 1970), 58-83.

71. Fusfeld, Daniel R. "The Economy of the Urban Ghetto." In John P. Crecine, editor. FINANCING THE METROPOLIS. Vol. 4, Urban Affairs Annual Reviews, Beverly Hills, Cal.: Sage Publications, 1970, 369-399.

72. Galenson, Marjorie, "Do Blacks Save More?" AMERICAN ECONOMIC REVIEW 62 (March 1972), 211-216.

73. Gans, Herbert. "Malemployment: The Problem of Underpaid and Dirty Work." NEW GENERATION 50 (Winter 1968), 15-18.

74. Gerson, Earle J. "Methodological and Interviewing Problems in Household Surveys of Employment Problems in Urban Poverty Neighborhoods." AMERICAN STATISTICAL ASSOCIATION PROCEEDINGS, 1969, Social Statistics Section, pp. 19-23.

75. Ginzberg, Eli. Testimony in EMPLOYMENT AND MANPOWER PROBLEMS IN THE CITY, Hearings before the Joint Economic Committee, Congress of the United States, 90 Congress, 2 Session, May 28-June 6, 1968, 120-124.

76. Gordon, David M. ECONOMIC THEORIES OF POVERTY AND DISCRIMINATION. New York: National Bureau of Economic Research, January 1971. Draft copy.

77. Gordon, David M. "Income and Welfare in New York City." PUBLIC INTEREST 16 (Summer 1969), 64-88.

78. Gordon, David M., editor. PROBLEMS IN POLITICAL ECONOMY: AN URBAN PERSPECTIVE. Lexington, Mass.: D.C. Heath, 1971.

79. Grebler, Leo. HOUSING MARKET BEHAVIOR IN A DECLINING AREA. New York: Columbia University Press, 1952.

80. Grubb, W. Norton. "The Distribution of Costs and Benefits in an Urban Public School System." NATIONAL TAX JOURNAL 24 (March 1971), 1-12.

81. Gwartney, James. "Discrimination and Income Differentials." AMERICAN ECONOMIC REVIEW 60 (June 1970), 396-408.

82. Haddad, William F., and G. Douglas Pugh, editors. BLACK ECONOMIC DEVELOPMENT. Englewood Cliffs, N.J.: Prentice-Hall, 1969.

83. Hanunian, Norman. THE ACCESSIBILITY OF PSYCHIATRIC OUTPATIENT CLINICS AND THEIR USE IN NEW YORK CITY.

84. D-19841-NYC, The NYC Rand Institute, January 2, 1970. Draft copy.
Hanushek, Eric A., and John F. Kain, "On the Value of *Equality of Educational Opportunity* as a Guide to Public Policy." In Frederick Mosteller and Daniel P. Moynihan, editors. ON EQUALITY OF EDUCATIONAL OPPORTUNITY. New York: Random House, 1972. Pp. 116-145.

85. Harries, Keith D. "Minority-Based Variations in Business Scale and Function: A Land-Use Analysis in Los Angeles, California." LAND ECONOMICS 48 (February 1972), 72-75.

86. Harrison, Bennett. "The Dual Economy and Public Service Employment." College Park: University of Maryland, July 1971. Mimeo.

87. Harrison, Bennett, EDUCATION, TRAINING AND THE URBAN GHETTO. Ph.D. dissertation. Philadelphia: University of Pennsylvania, 1970.

88. Harrison, Bennett. "Suburbanization and Ghetto Dispersal: A Critique of

the Conventional Wisdom." College Park: University of Maryland, July 1970. Mimeo.

89. Harsanyi, John C. "Approaches to the Bargaining Problem Before and After the Theory of Games: A Critical Discussion of Zeuthen's, Hicks', and Nast's Theories." ECONOMETRICA 24 (April 1956), 144-157.

90. Hefferin, E.A. A STUDY OF UTILIZATION BY BROOKLYN RESIDENTS OF PUBLICLY SUPPORTED MENTAL HOSPITALS DURING FISCAL YEARS 1965-1968, D-201123-NYC. NYC Rand Institute, April 29, 1970.

91. Heinberg, J.D., and W.E. Oates. "The Incidence of Differential Property Taxes on Urban Housing: A Comment and Some Further Evidence." NATIONAL TAX JOURNAL 23 (1970), 92-98.

92. Helper, Rose. RACIAL POLICIES AND PRACTICES OF REAL ESTATE BROKERS. Minneapolis: University of Minnesota Press, 1969.

93. Herbers, John. A series of articles in the NEW YORK TIMES, February 9, 1970, p. 35; January 2, 1972, pp. 1, 44; January 13, 1972, p. 35.

94. Hirsch, Werner Z. THE ECONOMICS OF STATE AND LOCAL GOVERN-MENT. New York: McGraw-Hill, 1970.

95. Hirsch, Werner Z., editor. ELEMENTS OF REGIONAL ACCOUNTS. Baltimore: Johns Hopkins Press, 1964.

96. Hirsch, Werner Z., editor. REGIONAL ACCOUNTS FOR POLICY DE-CISIONS. Baltimore: Johns Hopkins Press, 1966.

97. Hochwald, Werner, "Conceptual Issues of Regional Income Estimation." NBER STUDIES IN INCOME AND WEALTH. Princeton: Princeton University Press, 1957. Vol. 21, pp. 9-26.

98. Hochwald, Werner, editor. DESIGN OF REGIONAL ACCOUNTS. Baltimore: Johns Hopkins Press, 1961.

99. Housing and Development Administration of the City of New York. THE MAXIMUM BASE RENTS FORMULA, 1972.

100. Hughes, Graham. "Reparations for Blacks?" NEW YORK UNIVERSITY LAW REVIEW 43 (December 1968), 1063-1074.

101. Hunter, David R. THE SLUMS: CHALLENGE AND RESPONSE. New York: Free Press, 1964.

102. Isard, Walter. METHODS OF REGIONAL ANALYSIS: AN INTRO-DUCTION TO REGIONAL SCIENCE, Cambridge: M.I.T. Press, 1960.

103. Jaszi, George. "The Conceptual Basis of the Accounts: a Re-examination." NBER STUDIES IN INCOME AND WEALTH. Princeton: Princeton University Press, 1958. Vol. 22, pp. 13-127.

104. Johnson, Thomas A. "Numbers Called Harlem's Balm." NEW YORK TIMES, March 1, 1971, pp. 1, 42.

105. Johnston, Denis F., and James R. Wetzel. "Effect of the Census Under-count on Labor Force Estimates." MONTHLY LABOR REVIEW (March 1969), 3-13.

106. Kain, John F. "Housing Segregation, Negro Employment, and Metropoli-

tan Decentralization." QUARTERLY JOURNAL OF ECONOMICS 82 (May 1968), 175-197.

107. Kain, John F., and Joseph J. Persky. "Alternatives to the Gilded Ghetto." PUBLIC INTEREST 14 (Winter 1969), 74-87.

108. Kain, John F., and John M. Quigley. "Housing Market Discrimination, Home Ownership, and Savings Behavior." Paper prepared for American Economic Association meetings, December 1969. Mimeo.

109. Kain, John F., and John M. Quigley. "Measuring the Value of Housing Quality." JOURNAL OF THE AMERICAN STATISTICAL ASSOCIA-TION 55, 330 (June 1970), 532-548.

110. Keynes, John Maynard. THE GENERAL THEORY OF EMPLOYMENT, INTEREST AND MONEY. New York: Harcourt, Brace, and World, 1965.

111. Kotler, Milton. NEIGHBORHOOD GOVERNMENT. New York: Bobbs-Merill, 1969.

112. Kristof, Frank S. "Housing: Economic Facets of New York City's Problems." In Lyle C. Fitch and Annmarie Hauck Walsh, editors. AGENDA FOR CITY, Beverly Hills, Cal.: Sage Publications, 1970. Pp. 297-348.

113. Kuznets, Simon. NATIONAL INCOME AND ITS COMPOSITION. New York: National Bureau of Economic Research, 1941.

114. Lapham, Victoria. "Do Blacks Pay More for Housing?" JOURNAL OF POLITICAL ECONOMY 79 (November-December 1971), 1244-1257.

115. Lasswell, Harold, Jeromiah McKenna, and Mary Manoni. THE IMPACT OF ORGANIZED CRIME ON AN INNER CITY COMMUNITY. New York: The Policy Sciences Center, 1972. Draft Copy.

116. Leontief, Wassily. "Theoretical Assumptions and Nonobserved Facts." AMERICAN ECONOMIC REVIEW 61 (March 1972) 1-7.

117. Leven, Charles L. "Regional and Interregional Accounts in Perspective." REGIONAL SCIENCE ASSOCIATION, PAPERS AND PROCEEDINGS 13 (1964), 127-144.

118. Leven, Charles L. "Regional Income and Product Accounts: Construction and Application." In Werner Hochwald, editor, DESIGN OF REGIONAL ACCOUNTS. Baltimore: Johns Hopkins Press, 1961, pp. 148-195.

119. Lieberson, Stanley. ETHNIC PATTERNS IN AMERICAN CITIES. New York: Free Press, 1963.

120. Liebow, Elliot. TALLY'S CORNER, Boston: Little, Brown, 1967.

121. Lilley, William, III, and Timothy B. Clark. "Federal Programs Spur Abandonment of Housing in Major Cities." NATIONAL JOURNAL 4 (1972), 26-33.

122. Long, Norton E. "The City as Reservation." PUBLIC INTEREST 25 (Fall 1971), 22-38.

123. Lowry, Ira S. "Filtering and Housing Standards: A Conceptual Analysis." In Alfred Page and Warren Seyfried, editors. URBAN ANALYSIS. Glen-view, Ill.: Scott, Foresman, 1970. Pp. 339-347.

124. Lowry, Ira S., editor. RENTAL HOUSING IN NEW YORK CITY. Vol. I, "Confronting the Crisis." RM-6190-NYC, New York: NYC Rand Institute, February 1970.

125. McEntire, Davis. RESIDENCE AND RACE. Los Angeles: University of California Press, 1960.

126. McLauren, Dunbar S. GHEDIPLAN: GHETTO ECONOMIC DEVELOPMENT AND INDUSTRIALIZATION PLAN. New York City: Human Resources Administration, April 1968.

127. McPherson, James A. "In My Father's House There Are Many Mansions—And I'm Going to Get Me Some of Them Too: The Story of the Contract Buyers League." THE ATLANTIC MONTHLY 229 (April 1972), 51-82.

128. Malcolm X. THE AUTOBIOGRAPHY OF MALCOLM X. New York: Grove Press, 1964.

129. Margolis, Julius. "The Demand for Urban Public Services." In Harvey S. Perloff and Lowdon Wingo, Jr., editors. ISSUES IN URBAN ECONOMICS. Baltimore: Johns Hopkins Press, 1968. Pp. 527-564.

130. Marquez, Camilo. MUNICIPAL EXPENDITURES BY NEIGHBORHOOD. City of New York: Office of the Mayor, 1972.

131. Mason, Anthony. BLACK CAPITALISM. New York: Equity Research Associates, 1969.

132. Mayor's Task Force. THE ECONOMIC REDEVELOPMENT OF HARLEM. New York City: January 15, 1968.

133. Mellor, Earl F. "Public Goods and Services: Costs and Benefits—A Study of the Shaw-Cardoza Area of Washington, D.C." Institute for Policy Studies. Washington, D.C.: October 31, 1969.

134. Merton, Robert K. SOCIAL THEORY AND SOCIAL STRUCTURE. Glencoe, Ill.: Free Press, 1957.

135. Meyer, Harry, and Marvin Lansky. CHARACTERISTICS OF THE IN-PATIENT POPULATIONS SERVED BY THE NEW YORK CITY MUNICIPAL HOSPITALS, BOROUGH OF BROOKLYN. New York City Department of Hospitals, 1968.

136. Mieszkowski, Peter. "Tax Incidence Theory: The Effects of Taxes on the Distribution of Income." JOURNAL OF ECONOMIC LITERATURE 7 (December 1969), 1103-1124.

137. Mishan, E.J. "The Postwar Literature on Externalities: An Interpretative Essay." JOURNAL OF ECONOMIC LITERATURE 9 (March 1971), 1-28.

138. Mishan, E.J. "A Survey of Welfare Economics 1939-1959." ECONOMIC JOURNAL 70, 278 (June 1960), 197-264.

139. Mitchell, Daniel B. "Black Economic Development and Income Drain." REVIEW OF BLACK POLITICAL ECONOMY 1 (Autumn 1970), 47-56.

140. Moore, Samuel B. "Brooklyn—Past and Present." BROOKLYN LIFE 51, 1317 (May 29, 1915), 35-71.

141. Morgenstern, Oskar. ON THE ACCURACY OF ECONOMIC OBSERVATIONS. Princeton, N.J.: Princeton University Press, 1963.

142. Morrill, Richard L. "The Negro Ghetto: Problems and Alternatives." GEOGRAPHICAL REVIEW 55 (July 1965), 339-361.

143. Morrill, Richard L., and O. Fred Donaldson. "Geographical Perspectives on the History of Black America." ECONOMIC GEOGRAPHY 48 (January 1972), 1-23.

144. National Bureau of Economic Research. STUDIES IN INCOME AND WEALTH. Princeton: Princeton University Press, 1957-1958. Vols. 21, 22.

145. National Committee Against Discrimination in Housing. JOBS AND HOUSING: INTERIM REPORT. New York, March 1970.

146. Netzer, Dick. ECONOMICS OF THE PROPERTY TAX. Washington, D.C.: Brookings Institution, 1966.

147. New York City Planning Commission. PLAN FOR NEW YORK CITY. 6 vols. Cambridge, Mass.: M.I.T. Press, 1969.

148. New York City Planning Commission. "The Structure of Retail Activity in Slums." 1970. Mimeo.

149. Niedercorn, John. "A Neo-Mercantilist Model for Maximizing Ghetto Income." REVIEW OF BLACK POLITICAL ECONOMY 1 (Winter-Spring 1971), 22-27.

150. Oakland, William, Thomas Sparrow, and H. Louis Stettler, III. "Ghetto Multipliers—A Case Study of Hough." PROCEEDINGS of the Second Annual Research Conference of the Inter-University Committee on Urban Economics, September 1970, 159-181.

151. Oates, Wallace. "The Effects of Property Values: An Empirical Study of Tax Capitalization and the Tiebout Hypothesis." JOURNAL OF POLITICAL ECONOMY 77 (1969), 957-971.

152. O'Conner, James. "The Meaning of Economic Imperialism." In Robert I. Rhodes, editor, IMPERIALISM AND UNDERDEVELOPMENT. New York: Monthly Review Press, 1970. Pp. 101-150.

153. Ofari, Earl. THE MYTH OF BLACK CAPITALISM. New York: Monthly Review Press, 1970.

154. Office of Economic Opportunity. "Opportunity Funding—An Economic Development Demonstration Program." Washington, D.C.: OEO, March-April 1970.

155. Offner, Paul. LABOR FORCE PARTICIPATION IN THE GHETTO: A STUDY OF NEW YORK CITY POVERTY. Ph.D. dissertation, Princeton, N.J.: Princeton University, 1970.

156. Oldman, Oliver, and Henry Aaron. "Assessment—Sales Ratios Under the Boston Property Tax." NATIONAL TAX JOURNAL 18 (March 1965), 36-49.

157. Olson, Edgar O. "A Competitive Theory of the Housing Market." AMERICAN ECONOMIC REVIEW 59 (September 1969), 612-621.

158. Olson, Mancur. "Evaluating Performance in the Public Sector." CONFERENCE ON RESEARCH ON INCOME AND WEALTH. New York: National Bureau of Economic Research, November 4-6, 1971. Mimeo.

159. Olson, Mancur, and Christopher K. Clague. "Dissent in Economics: The Convergence of Extremes." SOCIAL RESEARCH 38 (Winter 1971) 751-776.

160. Orr, Larry L. "The Incidence of Differential Property Taxes on Urban Housing," NATIONAL TAX JOURNAL 21 (1968), 253-262.

161. Orr, Larry L. "The Incidence of Differential Property Taxes: A Reply." NATIONAL TAX JOURNAL 23 (1970), 99-101.

162. Osofsky, Gilbert. HARLEM: THE MAKING OF A GHETTO. New York: Harper & Row, 1968.

163. Pechman, Joseph A., Henry J. Aaren, and Michael K. Taussig. SOCIAL SECURITY: PERSPECTIVES FOR REFORM. Washington, D.C.: Brookings Institution, 1968.

164. Piven, Francis Fox, and Richard Cloward. REGULATING THE POOR. New York: Patheon, 1971.

165. Polytechnic Institute of Brooklyn. CENTRAL BROOKLYN MODEL CITIES AREA: TRANSPORTATION NEEDS OF RESIDENTS. New York, April 23, 1971.

166. President's National Advisory Panel on Insurance in Riot-Affected Areas. MEETING THE INSURANCE CRISIS OF OUR CITIES. Washington, D.C.: Government Printing Office, 1968.

167. Ranis, Gustav. "Economic Dualism—At Home and Abroad." PUBLIC POLICY 18 (Fall 1969), 41-54.

168. Rapoport, A., and C. Orwant. "Experimental Games: A Review." In Martin Shubik, editor. GAME THEORY AND RELATED APPROACHES TO SOCIAL BEHAVIOR. New York: Wiley, 1964. Pp. 283-310.

169. Rapping, Leonard A. "Union-Induced Racial Entry Barriers." JOURNAL OF HUMAN RESOURCES 5 (Fall 1970), 447-474.

170. Ratchford, B.U., and P.B. Han. "The Burden of the Corporate Income Tax." NATIONAL TAX JOURNAL 10 (December 1957), 310-324.

171. Richman, Raymond L. "The Incidence of Urban Real Estate Taxes Under Conditions of Static and Dynamic Equilibrium." LAND ECONOMICS 43 (May 1967), 172-180.

172. Rivlin, Alice. SYSTEMATIC THINKING FOR SOCIAL ACTION. Washington, D.C.: Brookings Institution, 1971.

173. Rose, Harold M. "The Spatial Development of Black Residential Subsystems." ECONOMIC GEOGRAPHY 48 (January 1972), 43-65.

174. Rothenberg, Jerome. ECONOMIC EVALUATION OF URBAN RENEWAL. Washington, D.C.: Brookings Institution, 1967.

175. Rubner, Alex. THREE SACRED COWS OF ECONOMICS. New York: Barnes and Noble, 1970.

176. Rust Engineering Company. REPORT ON THE FEASIBILITY OF ESTABLISHING A NEW STATE-CHARTERED BANK IN THE HILL DISTRICT OF PITTSBURGH, PENNSYLVANIA. March 14, 1968.

177. Samuelson, Paul A. "The Pure Theory of Public Expenditures." REVIEW OF ECONOMICS AND STATISTICS 36 (November 1954), 387-389.

178. Sawers, Larry. THE LABOR FORCE PARTICIPATION OF THE URBAN POOR. Ph.D. dissertation. Ann Arbor: University of Michigan, 1969.

179. Scheiner, Seth. NEGRO MECCA: A HISTORY OF THE NEGRO IN NEW YORK CITY 1865-1920. New York: New York University Press, 1965.

180. Schiller, Bradley. "Stratified Opportunities: The Essence of the 'Vicious Circle.' " AMERICAN JOURNAL OF SOCIOLOGY 76 (November 1970), 426-442.

181. Schreiberg, Sheldon. "Home Ownership for Tenants: A Program to Use Tax-Foreclosed Properties." HARVARD JOURNAL OF LEGISLATION 7 (November 1969), 67-120.

182. Sen, Amartya K. "Isolation, Assurances and the Social Rate of Discount." QUARTERLY JOURNAL OF ECONOMICS 80 (February 1967), 112-124.

183. Sexton, Donald E. "Comparing the Cost of Food to Blacks and to Whites—a Survey." JOURNAL OF MARKETING 35 (July 1971), 40-46.

184. Shapiro, Harvey D. FIRE INSURANCE AND THE INNER CITY. R-703-NSF. New York: Rand Institute, February 1971.

185. Small Business Administration. CRIME AGAINST SMALL BUSINESS. Washington, D.C.: Government Printing Office, April 3, 1969.

186. Smolensky, Eugene, Selwyn Becker, and Harvey Molotch. "The Prisoner's Dilemma and Ghetto Expansion." LAND ECONOMICS 44 (November 1968), 419-430.

187. Spear, Allan H. BLACK CHICAGO: THE MAKING OF A NEGRO GHETTO 1890-1920. Chicago: University of Chicago Press, 1967.

188. Sporn, Arthur. "Empirical Studies in the Economics of Slum Ownership." LAND ECONOMICS 36 (November 1960), 333-340.

189. Spratlen, Thaddeus. "Ghetto Economic Development: The Character and Content of the Literature." Paper prepared for the 1970 Workshop of the Caucus of Black Economists, Chicago, September 18, 1970. Mimeo.

190. Stegman, Michael A., "The New Mythology of Housing." TRANSACTION 7 (January 1970), 55-62.

191. Sternlieb, George. THE TENEMENT LANDLORD. New Brunswick, N.J.: Rutgers University Press, 1969.

192. Sternlieb, George. THE URBAN HOUSING DILEMMA. New Brunswick, N.J.: Center for Urban Social Science Research, Rutgers University, 1970.

193. Sturdivant, Frederick. "The Limits of Black Capitalism." HARVARD BUSINESS REVIEW (January-February 1969), 122-128.

194. Sturdivant, Frederick, and William Hauselman. "Discrimination in the Marketplace: Another Dimension." SOCIAL SCIENCE QUARTERLY 52 (December 1971), 625-630.

195. Suttles, Gerald. THE SOCIAL ORDER OF THE SLUM. Chicago: University of Chicago Press, 1968. 196.

196. Tabb, William K. THE POLITICAL ECONOMY OF THE BLACK GHETTO. New York: W.W. Norton, 1970.

197. Taeuber, Karl, and Alma. NEGROES IN CITIES. Chicago: Aldine, 1965.

198. Taylor, Elizabeth K., and Arthur C. Wolfe. "The Problem of Completeness of Sample Coverage." In John B. Lansing, Stephen B. Withey, and Arthur C. Wolfe, editors. WORKING PAPERS ON SURVEY RESEARCH IN POVERTY AREAS. Ann Arbor, Michigan: Survey Research Center, University of Michigan, January 1971, 1-25.

199. Terrell, Henry. THE FISCAL IMPACT OF NEGROES ON CENTRAL CITIES. Ph.D. dissertation. Palo Alto, Cal.: Stanford University, 1969.

200. Thurow, Lester. POVERTY AND DISCRIMINATION. Washington, D.C.: Brookings Institution, 1969.

201. Tiebout, Charles M. THE COMMUNITY ECONOMIC BASE STUDY. Supplementary Paper #16. New York: Committee for Economic Development, 1962.

202. Tiebout, Charles M. "Community Income Multipliers: A Population Growth Model." JOURNAL OF REGIONAL SCIENCE 2 (Spring 1960), 75-84.

203. Tiebout, Charles M. "A Pure Theory of Local Expenditures." JOURNAL OF POLITICAL ECONOMY 64 (1956), 416-424.

204. United States Department of Commerce, Bureau of the Census. EMPLOYMENT PROFILES OF SELECTED LOW-INCOME AREAS, BROOKLYN BOROUGH, NYC—AREA II. PHC (3)-9. Washington, D.C.: Government Printing Office, January 1972.

205. United States Department of Labor. MANPOWER REPORT OF THE PRESIDENT 1971. Washington, D.C.: Government Printing Office, 1971.

206. United States Department of Labor. "Pilot and Experimental Program on Urban Employment Surveys." Report #354. Washington, D.C.: Government Printing Office, March 1969.

207. United States Department of Labor. "A Sharper Look at Unemployment in U.S. Cities and Slums." Washington, D.C.: Government Printing Office, 1967.

208. United States Senate, Report of PROCEEDINGS, Hearings Held before Subcommittee on Antitrust and Monopoly of the Committee on the Judiciary, COMPETITION IN REAL ESTATE AND MORTGAGE LENDING AS IT AFFECTS THE HOUSING CRISIS. 3 vols. of testimony in transcript form. Boston, September 13-15, 1971.

209. Vietorisz, Thomas, and Bennett Harrison. THE ECONOMIC DEVELOPMENT OF HARLEM. New York: Praeger, 1970.

210. Vietorisz, Thomas, and Bennett Harrison. A PROPOSED INVESTMENT PROGRAM FOR THE ECONOMIC DEVELOPMENT OF CENTRAL HARLEM. 2 vols. New York: Center for Economic Planning of the New School for Social Research, June 30, 1968.

211. Walker, Mable. URBAN PLIGHT AND SLUMS. Cambridge: Harvard University Press, 1938.
212. Wallich, Henry, and William J. Dodson. "Economic Models and Black Economic Development." Paper prepared for the American Economic Association meetings, December 1969.
213. Weaver, Robert C. THE NEGRO GHETTO. New York: Russell and Russell, 1948.
214. Weicher, John C. "The Allocation of Police Protection by Income Class." URBAN STUDIES 8 (October 1971), 207-220.
215. Weicher, John C. "Determinants of Central City Expenditure: Some Overlooked Factors and Problems." NATIONAL TAX JOURNAL 23 (December 1970), 379-396.
216. Weicher, John C. "The Effect of Urban Renewal on Municipal Service Expenditures." JOURNAL OF POLITICAL ECONOMY 80 (January-February 1972), 86-101.
217. Westinghouse Learning Corporation. AN EVALUATION OF FISCAL YEAR 1968 SPECIAL IMPACT PROGRAMS: Vol. 6—BEDFORD-STUY-VESANT. Bladensburg, Maryland, July 31, 1970.
218. Williams, Walter. "Cleveland's Crisis Ghetto." TRANSACTION 4 (September 1967), 33-42.
219. Wright, Robert A. "Watts 1970: Despite Changes, Much Remains the Same Five Years After Riots." NEW YORK TIMES, September 13, 1970. P. 80.
220. Zweig, Michael. "Black Capitalism and the Ownership of Property in Harlem." Working Paper #16, N.Y.: State University of New York at Stony Brook, August 1970.

Index

Index

About the Author

Richard Schaffer is currently an economic consultant to the Bedford-Stuyvesant Restoration Corporation, where he is engaged in further economic research on the Bedford-Stuyvesant community. He received his B.S. from the Wharton School of the University of Pennsylvania in 1969, and his Ph.D. in economics from New York University in 1972.